By the Word of Their Testimony

"And they overcame him because of the
blood of the Lamb and because of the
word of their testimony…"
Revelation 12:11

He will Give You the Desires of Your Heart

Book 5

Cover Design by Dallas & Tara Thiele • NarrowRoad Publishing House

By the Word of Their Testimony

He will Give You the Desires of Your Heart

Published by:
NarrowRoad Publishing House
POB 830
Ozark, MO 65721 U.S.A.

The materials from Restore Ministries were written for the sole purpose of encouraging women. For more information, please take a moment to visit us at: **www.EncouragingWomen.org or www.RestsoreMinistries.net.**

Unless otherwise indicated, most Scripture verses are taken from the *New American Standard Bible* (NASB). Scripture quotations marked KJV are taken from the *King James Version* of the Bible, and Scripture quotations marked NIV are taken from the *New International Version.* Our ministry is not partial to any particular version of the Bible but **love** them all so that we are able to help every woman in any denomination who needs encouragement and who has a desire to gain greater intimacy with her Savior.

Library of Congress Control number: 2018903779
ISBN: 1-931800-38-3
ISBN 13: 978-1-931800-38-9

Contents

Introduction

Your Divine Appointment

"I was **crying** to the LORD with my voice,
And He **answered me** from His holy mountain"
—Psalm 3:4.

Have you been searching for marriage help? It's not by chance, nor is it by coincidence, that you are reading this book. God has heard your cry for help in your marriage dilemma. He predestined this DIVINE APPOINTMENT to give you the hope that you so desperately need right now!

If you have been told that your marriage is hopeless or that without your spouse's help your marriage cannot be restored, then this is the book you need. Read this over and over so you will begin to believe that God is MORE than able to restore ANY marriage, including YOURS!

We know and understand what you are going through since WE, and MANY others who have come to our ministry for help, have a restored marriage and family! No matter what others have told you, your marriage is NOT hopeless!! We KNOW, after twenty five years of ministry, that God is able to restore ANY marriage, even YOURS!

If you have been crying out to God for more help, someone who understands, then join our Internet Restoration Fellowship Online and you'll receive an ePartner (email partner) who will help you see your marriage through to restoration during your rebuilding phase of your journey. Since beginning this fellowship, we have seen more marriages restored on a regular basis than we ever thought possible!

So, if you are really serious in your desire to restore your marriage, then our fellowship is the answer. For more information or to join, go to our website RMIEW.com. We would love for you to be a part of our Restoration Fellowship!

Who are we and what are we hoping to do?

Restore Ministries helps those who have found themselves in a hopeless situation: couples whose spouse is in adultery, has left, has filed for divorce, or any other seemingly impossible marital situation. These broken people have often sought help, but everyone (many times even their pastors) have told them their marriage was hopeless. However, we not only believe that no marriage is hopeless – regardless of the circumstances—we know they aren't. That's why we offer hope, help and encouragement through our website, our Restoration Fellowship, and a variety of resources including a variety of newsletters to spiritual feed and uplift you daily!

In 2001, Restoration Fellowship was birthed to minister more effectively to the needs of those seriously seeking restoration. Within a year the fellowship grew to over 400 committed members and increases daily with members from all over the world.

Restore Ministries has never sought advertising or paid for placement in search engines but has instead grown by word of mouth. We also take no support from anyone but the individuals themselves who are seeking restoration so that we are never told we must comprise sharing His full truths. Though often ostracized by the established church, because of those who have cried out to God for help when their own church, pastor, family and friends who offered them no hope or support, we have given them hope and we have become an oasis in the desert for the desperate, the hurting, the rejected.

Often accused of being extreme, radical, out-of-balance or legalistic, the message in all our resources is founded firmly on the Word of God only, encouraging those seeking restoration to live the message that Jesus proclaimed, beginning with the familiar Beatitudes.

RMI teaches the good news of God's Word to bring healing to the brokenhearted, comfort to those in pain, and freedom to prisoners of despondency and sin through the truth of His Word, giving them the hope that is "against all hope" through the Power of Jesus Christ, the Mighty Counselor and Good Shepherd.

Our site and our resources minister to the hurting all over the world with the intent of creating a deeper and more intimate walk with the Lord that results in the hurting healed, the bound freed, the naked clothed, the lost saved and broken marriages restored. We minister to women from more than 15 countries including Switzerland, Hong Kong, New Zealand, Sweden,

Philippines, Brazil and Germany, with large followings in Australia, Canada, and Africa. Our books have been translated into Spanish, Portuguese, Tagalog (Filipino), Afrikaans, and French. Also Slovakian, Chinese, Russian, Italian and some Hindi.

Jesus said that you "will know them by their fruits" that's why this book and all our *By the Word of Their Testimony* books are filled with testimonies of hopeless marriages that were restored, marriages that give glory to God and to the Power of His Word. Our *WOTT* books are growing at such a phenomenal rate that we were once unable to keep up with getting them published. Now we have a full team devoted to keeping up.

If you have any doubt about the validly of our ministry, you won't after reading this and our other awesome books. Each will show you not only hopeless marriages that were restored, but more importantly, it will show you men and women who have been completely transformed into God-lovers and are now committed on-fire Christians, many of whom were saved through this ministry.

Below is a small sampling of the letters of gratitude that Restore Ministries has received. Please note when you read the letters that they give all the praise and glory to the Lord. This ministry was founded and continues to grow on the premise that "if He be lifted up, He will draw all men to Himself" and "the Lord will share His glory with no man."

"Let Another Praise You" Proverbs 27:2

I want to thank this ministry for all the support they are giving me and my RJ. I am finding I am not so focused on my Marriage as I am with doing the will of My Lord. This ministry has been pivotal in my journey and my walk with Christ. I am so grateful that I was able to find some where that would give me the resources to find my place with My Lord. I just want another woman to feel the joy and the peace that I have had with this ministry.

I was at the end of my rope, I did not care if I lived or died as my life was so changed by my EH walking out on me. This ministry saved my life. If it does anything at all it pointed me in the right direction to My Lord.

It helped me see that it was my relationship with him that mattered. No human Man can give you what My Lord can give you, No human Man can fill your heart the way My Lord can. It is important for all areas of your life to know that He is here and he will always be here.

~ *Laurence in Canada*

THANK You!! I am currently on my own restoration journey for my marriage and this is the most incredible journey. I have learned so many different things about myself and what God is doing and has been doing for me. I have grown up in a time that seemed simple and right yet when my life came crashing down around me I struggled. Nearly one year later I found a RYM book (and I will never know how the information ended up in my hands) and I truly believe it was God who led me to your ministry. My life has changed completely. God is wonderful. He is providing for me each and every single day.

When I found RMI I had been separated for approximately a year. I was pursuing and was contentious. Wow, how things have changed and how much I love the changes! I have a calmness now knowing that God is in control of my life.

Thank you so very much for everything. God has used you to help change me. Thank you for being one of God's prophets and for what you are doing for me.

~ *Laurie in Florida*

Thank You to everyone at RMI. Your online courses have helped me to see all I had done in the break down of my marriage. and what I need to do to correct my short coming and become the kind of wife the Lord wanted me to be. I tell every women I come into contact with that is having marriage problems about the RYM book and your ministry, it has been a Godsend for me as I work toward knowing the Lord as my Husband. And also to your partners.

My husband just packed everything up and left one day while I was at work, leaving the state. I did'nt hear from him for 6 months. I was so fillied with hurt, anger and pain. I wanted my husband and my marriage I did'nt understand what was so bad that he felt he had to do what he did the way he did it.

It was that pain that lead me to the internet looking for help on restoring my marriage. Again, I would like to thank all of you. I will give your books to hurting women I come accross in need but I also try to get some in our local library.

Thank You again for the books!!

~ Alisa in Florida

We put this book and all our *Word of Their Testimony* books together because we believe that as you spend some time reading these incredible and awesome testimonies of seemingly hopeless marriages that were miraculously restored, you will be encouraged and know without a doubt...

NOTHING IS IMPOSSIBLE WITH GOD!!

Nothing is Impossible
with God!

"Looking at them, Jesus said,
'With people it is impossible,
but not with God;
for all things are possible with God.'"
Mark 10:27

*"And they overcame him because of the blood of the Lamb and because of the **word of THEIR testimony**, and they did not love their life even to death." Rev. 12:11.*

The following testimonies are filled with miracles of men and women who took God at His Word and believed that "nothing was impossible with God!" Those who have had the miracle of a restored marriage have several things in common. All "delighted themselves in the Lord" and He gave them "the desires of their heart." All of them "hoped against hope" when their situation seemed hopeless.

All of them "fought the good fight" and "finished their course." All of them were determined "not to be overcome with evil" but instead to "overcome evil with good." All were willing to "bless their enemies" and to pray for them that "despitefully used and persecuted them." All "turned the other cheek" and "walked the extra mile." All realized that it was "God who removed lover and friend far from" them and it was God who "made them a loathing" to their spouse. All of them understood and believed that it is NOT the will of man (or woman) but the "will of God" who can "turn the heart" whichever way He chooses.

All refused to fight in "the flesh" but chose to battle "in the spirit." None were concerned to protect themselves, but trusted themselves "to Him who judges righteously." All of their trust was "in the Lord" because their trust was "the Lord." All released their attorneys (if that was part of their testing)

since they "would rather be wronged or defrauded." All of them "got out of the way of wickedness" and "let the unbeliever leave" since they "were called to peace." All refused to do "evil for evil or insult for insult." All loved their spouse who may have been unfaithful because they knew that "love never fails."

This is the same journey that the Lord took me on back in 1989. That year I made a promise to God that if He would restore my marriage to my husband, I would devote my life to telling others about Him and His desire and ability to restore ANY marriage no matter what the circumstances. The Lord was faithful and restored my marriage, suddenly, two years later after a divorce. (Yes! AFTER a divorce!) Now I faithfully, with the Lord's continued help, love, support, and guidance, spread the GOOD news that nothing—NOT A THING—is impossible with God!

It is important to know that our ministry was FOUNDED to help all those who were told by pastors and Christian friends that their situations were HOPELESS. Those who come to us for hope are facing a spouse who is deep in adultery, who has moved out (often in with the other man or woman who committed adultery with), who has already filed for divorce or whose divorce has gone through. 99% of those who come, come alone for help since their spouse is not interested in saving their marriage, but is desperately trying to get out. Over 95% claim that they are Christians and most are married to Christians.

Over half are in some type of Christian service and many of the men who are involved with other woman are pastors who have left not only their wife and children, but their church as well.

If you, or if someone you know, is facing devastation in their marriage, there is hope. Read these awesome testimonies that prove that God is MORE than able to restore ANY marriage

Chapter 1

Leonard & Janine

"Oh Lord, You took up my case;
You redeemed my life"
—Lamentations 3:58

"Remarried Sober After 15 Painful Years"

HIS Testimony

Fifteen years ago, things just went bad. Me and my wife argued a lot and we had a lot of single friends and started clubbing. My cousin said I must try this drug cocaine, which will make me feel better. I kept on saying no, and he kept on that it will make all my problems disappear. I gave in and started using cocaine. I said I didn't want Janine anymore, but that wasn't what my heart felt. A lady working at my sister's business overheard my mother and sister talking about me and Janine and how bad it was going between us. She started phoning me, and it was a lady I would never have previously looked at. She said I must go out with them, and I did. She made it easy for me with everything. She just did everything right and knew how to play it right.

Me and Janine started having boys nights and girls nights and we drifted further apart. I moved out at the end of that year, and I guess I wanted Janine to fight for me, but instead she gave me a number to get divorced for cheap and I thought that was what she wanted, so I got divorced just over a year later. I even went to church but it was to keep my father happy but it wasn't the right way, because Thursday to Sundays were my drug days whereby I would even stay awake for 3 days. It numbed the pain I had with Janine. From the beginning, I was sorry that we got divorced, but I kept on telling myself that Janine didn't worry about me. And the more Janine fought, the more I told myself I was doing the right thing.

The OW kept on buying me gifts and supporting me financially, and more and more my self-confidence disappeared. At first, the gifts comforted me, but later it didn't even comfort me for an hour. I started caring less and less. And the bad thing is I didn't tolerate anything wrong from the OW and she knew it. I asked her to marry me under the influence of drugs, and on our wedding day, I wasn't there for most of the reception because I was driving with my friend in his Ferrari. On our honeymoon, I phoned my parents to join us because I didn't want to be alone with her.

Holidays and Christmases were the most difficult times because I missed my family. I didn't want to go to places where me and Janine went because it was too painful. More and more I looked for a hobby to keep me busy and for me, it was drugs and gambling, and the OW provided for that. I didn't care about the stuff she bought me and sold it quickly for my bad habits, but the stuff Janine bought me I kept.

I couldn't even drive where me and Janine used to drive. I avoided places where me and Janine had gone to. And it was even terribly painful for me to just see her, it was like a knife in my heart if I saw her. I tried to keep myself busy the whole time, not to think, and it was with drugs and gambling, and if I wasn't on drugs I slept. Songs even reminded me of Janine. The OW was the easy way out, or so I thought. My personality changed even more and more. I went my own way and the OW didn't fight with me, I could even go away with Janine for a weekend and she would ask me if I enjoyed it. I did everything bad that would normally cause the OW to just leave me, but she didn't.

My advice to women waiting for their husbands would be, if he divorced you don't tease him and don't have intimacy with him because it was easy when I had my bread buttered on both sides, I didn't have to choose. And don't keep on texting him and phoning him, Janine did keep on and she didn't give me the time to miss her. The more you cling to the person the more you push that person away. The moment she stopped phoning, texting and being intimate with me and let go, things changed for me. The OW also started changing then, and when I saw the OW with another man it wasn't painful and it didn't worry me, and my sister even asked why didn't I confront her. But if it was Janine I would have beaten up the guy for. But don't go and get another guy because that is not the solution, it will make it just worse. I went back and forth with Janine but I was still on drugs, and I would fight for nothing with Janine.

On February 11 I just broke down and I know it was God that just brought me to my knees. God told me the only way I would get my family back is to go His way. I just wanted Janine by me and phoned her. At that time I lived by my mother and would have walked to Janine if she didn't come to talk to me. She came over and I cried and cried, and didn't even worry who looked at me. She held me and when I said I lost everything, she said no I didn't. I wanted to go with her to church because I saw a change in her. I even said to her, previously she wouldn't have forgiven me so quick. On February 14th I went with her to church and I won't ever turn back to drugs again. At the right time, God brought us back together. I wanted to get married quickly and we got married on March 11. The most important thing is to give everything over to God. God took away my selfishness, and with that my desire to use drugs. I always felt sorry for myself and that made me more selfish, and God even took that away because that also pushed me to use more drugs.

~ Leonard in Botswana

HER Testimony

Leonard was my school sweetheart. A year later, I walked away with him and wanted to spend the rest of my life with him. Two years later, I became pregnant with our first son and on December 6, we got married. He was 19 at the time and I was 21. The first 2 years were awesome, but the third year we started arguing more and more. We started clubbing and I felt I had my young life back again. We were married just three years when he came home and said he felt we needed to give our hearts to God, but I said no and that I was enjoying my life too much. He even came home once and asked that I help him because he started using drugs, but I was so full of myself that I said he must sort out his own mess, and if my parents were to find out I would divorce him.

I knew he was unfaithful to me and I wanted to take revenge and was unfaithful to him. When I went through his phone I found this one number and confronted the OW, but she replied that they were friends and there was nothing I could do about it. I just fought more and more and one night it went so bad he admitted he slept with a lady, and I was so furious I admitted I too slept with somebody else.

On December 1, just 3 months after we'd given our hearts to God, he moved out and I gave him a phone number to divorce me and I really didn't think he would go through with it. I just broke when he did and I started going to church but I didn't do it for the right reasons, I just wanted my husband back. I phoned and texted him and her like crazy. At a stage I even got involved with drugs and would drink 9 ecstasy pills and sniff coke at once, it was only God's grace that kept me alive!! I just felt worse and worse and went into depression and tried to kill myself, and when I was in the hospital, I let them phone Leonard to come and fetch me because I just wanted to be with him. He immediately came but I was so hurt I also just wanted to fight with him, but it just pushed him more and more away from me.

Leonard married the OW 3 years after I'd given the phone number to divorce me, and I also got a boyfriend and thought that would be the solution. Yes, it made him jealous, but it was the worst thing I could have done because if I had stayed on my knees in front of God, I know we would have been back together sooner. I didn't keep boyfriends long because my heart longed for my husband Leonard. My doctor said she had to admit me to a hospital for depression but I asked her to give me one week to sort out my life. I threw away the depression and sleeping pills and asked God to help me, and ever since been free from pills. Leonard went on going back and forth between me and OW and 2 years after Leonard married the OW, I became pregnant with his son, but I also kept on fighting with him because of how could he put me through it alone, and of course I made matters worse. The OW didn't leave him and just held on more to him. I would always say to him what if she became pregnant, and when we fought I would say to him I know she is going to become pregnant. And then, she did and they had a baby girl in November, 2 years after I'd had our son. It broke me and that's when I learned what power our words have. I stopped using drugs after getting pregnant with our baby boy and I tried to move closer to God. But still, I didn't stop phoning him and texting him. I begged him to come back but he wouldn't, and my fighting didn't stop.

Four years after me trying to move closer to God, I learned about "standing," I asked the ministry if I could stand for my marriage even after he was remarried and the reply was yes. I know I didn't do it right, standing, but the most of the time I was too busy with my own feelings. About a year later, I went to this new church where I started giving over more and more to God and it was a pastor that didn't believe in getting married again. Two years later I stopped with all the texting and phone calls and just let go of him and I started watching my words. Then about a year later, I got prophetic word from my pastor that God is going to give me my family back. I know if I had given everything over to God sooner my story would have been so different, but again I know I had to go through all the pain to warn others not to make the same mistakes I did. Give everything over to God from the start and let go from the start, don't you try and fix it with your own plans and schemes. I felt the OW starting losing interest in Leonard when I started giving over more and more to God and watched my words, and when I started talking less to other people about my situation and let him go.

Leonard started phoning me more and more and he even started saying he missed me more as soon as I let go. But he kept on using drugs, but I prayed more. On February 11, he phoned me and asked me to come and see him. I just felt I had to go, and at that stage, he just broke down. I held him in my arms and we cried together not even worrying who was looking at us. He said he had lost everything and I replied that he hadn't and that I just wanted him to get his life right with God and stop using drugs. He said he was finished with drugs and just wanted his family back and that he would go with me to church (which he previously said he would never do).

On February 14, he went with me to church, it was the best Valentine's Day ever, without gifts, but this time with God (oh yes but he gave me a chocolate with the words "I love you", which I still keep, I can't eat it, it's too special, lol). He wanted to get married again very quickly, and on March 11 of this year, we got married, and it was just us and our pastor and the kids, and of course God. A week before our wedding I said to God, this time I can lose Leonard, but I can't lose God and I know that was He has changed me because God is my first love now and will always be. A week after our wedding he said, "I know you feel shocked because this all happened very quickly, but get used to it because this is for life, and get used to my face because I am going to get old and you are stuck with me for life." He is such a changed person and I'm treated like a queen, and that is all because of God!

Don't let your own feelings get in the way of your restoration. Humble yourself to God and do it as quick as possible, not like I did it. A week before our wedding I got a beautiful vision from God: God showed me a very black thick curtain and that Satan wants us to think that it is a very thick wall and that there is no hope because of the darkness you see in front of you, but it's only a curtain and God is working behind that curtain and at the right time God will pull away the curtain so that you can see the beautiful picture God was working on, so don't believe Satan's lies. I know 15 years was a very long time, but if it can help only one other person not to make the same mistakes I did, then it was all worth it!!!

We still have so much to say but me and Leonard said bit by bit. We wanted to share more in our testimony but so much happened in those 15 painful years that we hoped would help encourage other couples.

~ Janine in Botswana

Janine's FRIEND

I praise the Lord for the restoration of this marriage. I think I am more pleased for my friend's restoration than I will ever be for my own:):):). He is so faithful and wonderful and the reason I am adding to this already amazing Restored Marriage testimony is because I was led to give my view from the outside.

So, I will start with my relationship with my dear friend because in this you will also see how our wonderful Heavenly Husband works. We used to work in the same building since 1999 and though I knew of her, I did not know her. Years later we met again in the building we are currently working in. We said Hi from time to time, but I never really felt comfortable in her company because she would speak so freely of the Lord, and I did not want to hear because I was not even sure that He really existed. And though I may not have been ready to hear the truth, the seed must have been planted because when my marriage fell apart, her name came up when I sat in church. So I went to her and she sowed the *How God Can and Will Restore Your Marriage* book in my life. She also gave me the Prison to Praise book.

Later she told me that she was talking to the Lord one morning on her way to work and asked Him for a true friend. Well, the Lord answered that prayer and so much more. In each other we found comfort and together we learned to turn to the Lord for everything we need.

As I was starting with the RMI and learning the principles of the Bible, I could see the Lord teaching them to my friend as well. I could see the wonderful change in her and ladies we all know that we have changed once the Lord gets hold of us:), but seeing the change in someone else is breathtakingly beautiful. From the first time I started reading the Bible, she made me think of David, because she had a heart for the Lord, and although she was not as obedient as she should have been, I could see a love for the Lord in her that made me crave Him even more.

My friend came from the background of a "stander" and if you have done the **Renew, Rebuild and Restore** online courses in this ministry, you will see the pitfalls within "standing", but for our wonderful Lord, nothing is impossible!!! So as my friend became closer to the Lord I could see her letting go of her then FH and I could see the Lord glowing out of her.

I cannot praise the Lord enough for what He did for my friend and to tell each one of you: "Be encouraged, what He did for her, He can and will do for you!!!!!!!!"

~Yvonne in Botswana

Chapter 2

Valerie

"Give all your cares to the Lord
and He will give you strength.
He will never let those who are
right with Him be shaken"
—Psalm 55:22

"Married to My Son's Father"

How did your restoration actually begin Valerie?

A week before my son's father had decided to put an end to our 9 years relationship as a common-law couple (i.e.when living together in a conjugal relationship for three years or more), I had asked God to release me from this relationship. We were not happy and we kept fighting and criticize each other.

God heard me and knew it was time for me to get a reality check.

The 2 years following that moment, there were a few moments when restoration could have happened if it was not for my many mistakes (and for God's appointed time of course).

When I came to this ministry looking for hope, I filled out my questionnaire saying, "I still think that there is hope." And why I was seeking restoration was "Because I think it is the best situation for my child."

And then, when the OW finally got out of the picture, my son's father started to try to get closer and he initiated moments for the three of us to spend together. We started to have dinner as a family a few times a week and to do activities on the weekend. He told me he wanted me to move in with him so that we could be a family once again. I had to tell him that this time, I would not have any relations with him until we would get married. This was the first time that he seemed to agree with the idea and even if he did not understand why I could not move in with him before the wedding day. This time I knew that I did not have to worry about it happening or not. I really let it all into His hands. I had let go and let God. I did though fear at times that I was still making so many mistakes and my biggest fear was to not be able to please Him at all times.

Valerie, how did God change your situation as you sought Him wholeheartedly?

God changed my situation by allowing so many things to happen in my favor, all that happened at the same time. He gave me work opportunities without having me to do much. He gave me a group of women at work with whom I was able to share a part of my testimonies and His word. He showered me with so many love songs and I have received more a double portion; instead of humiliation. When I've discovered music that suited me, so many things changed in my life. I was able to talk to Him while studying, waking up every morning singing to Him, walking to work and back home with songs in my ears. This music made it possible for me to spend more time with Him while having less time to sit, read and pray – I found a new way and I think that my situation changed a lot at that moment.

What principles, from God's Word (or through our resources), did the Lord teach you during this trial Valerie?

The first principle that still has an effect on everyone around me and that amazes family and friends, is the fact that I've let go of **legal and judicial aid and recourse**. Being a **student in law** and having parents and friends who are lawyers, I had to stand firm and the results were enormous.

The other main principle that made the restoration possible this time was the importance of marriage. At first, when I found out about the ministry, I thought that it would be really difficult to end up being married to my son's father. Because I had never been married, I was wondering if God had just released me from this relationship. It also took me a while before I stopped doubting that I could and should even be part of RMI and that its principles could apply to me. I had to learn from my disobedience and after a few attempts to restore my family without FIRST being married, I had to firmly believe that His ways were the only ways. And then, it all became so simple (in the last stretch at least ;).

My disobedience made my journey longer and that was all right. It allowed me to repent from all other mistakes I had made, and practice being quiet (which I still struggle a lot with every day), to have a gentle spirit instead.

I still struggle with contentment at times and I thank God He is still with me to fight fear.

Valerie, what were the most difficult times that God helped you through?

Apart from the difficulty to see my son hurt (and that was until my ePartner made me realize that it was a trap from the enemy) and to not be able to spend as much time with him, I've struggled the most with fear: fear of not doing the right thing, fear of not pleasing Him, fear of fearing, fear of not being ready for restoration, fear of making too many mistakes, fear of still being contentious, fear of the enemy in my house, and of course, fear to disappoint all my family in failing in my restoration etc.

Even today sometimes I need to be reminded that His grace is sufficient and that He has mercy for us each morning. It is the enemy who is making me doubt, he is making me think that I am doing everything wrong. I was also keeping myself from sharing good news with people around me. The enemy was making me think that I wasn't being humble and that I was bragging, which made me lack complete contentment in the eyes of others who were just waiting to see this miracle.

I know that I still need to stop doubting in EVERYTHING and LET HIM work His miracles.

Valerie what was the "turning point" of your restoration?

I had started to write my testimony *before* the wedding actually occurred, because this time I knew that fear had to be conquered in order for His will to be done. I was feared sharing the news of the engagement to my son's father, in case it would not really happen, but through all the summer, all the words I was reading reminded me to fight fear. I even broke my left hand 2 weeks before our wedding, I got really scared that God was telling me to stop. Again, it was fear and fear is the enemy. This feeling was also confirmed when I wrote to Erin (she's a close friend of our family), I heard Him telling me that of all the people that should learn my news, she deserved to know all the miracles that are due to this ministry. When she answered me, she sent me the testimony link, just like that. :)

It was my mother who started to send me the Encourager and she gave me the book *How God Can and Will Restore Your Marriage*

Tell us HOW it happened Valerie?

On my birthday, after telling my son's father all summer that I was not going to move in with him, that I was not even going to be his girlfriend without being married, he organized a dinner and just before we got there, he stopped the car and proposed to me. Two days later, I got in a bike accident and broke my hand and wasn't even able to walk for 2 weeks. Our wedding day was in 3 weeks and a week before I went back to the hospital to see how my hand was doing, the fracture had "disappeared"! This was another sign that I should not fear.

Valerie, did you suspect or could you tell you were close to being restored?

Yes, I could.

Would you recommend any of our resource in particular that helped you Valerie?

Everything.

The *How God Can and Will Restore Your Marriage* book and *By the Word of Their Testimony* were what I needed to realize that I should not move on to another life than the one I had started with my family. The RRR online courses made me stronger and Erin's Be Encouraged eVideos were essential when going to bed each night. I appreciate the fact that there is a resource that can be used for any moment or phase of our lives. Thank you!

Even though these are all designed for women who are married, the principles are basically the same even if you're not. When I filled out my free marriage evaluation, I asked this question: I have been reading the First Chapter of "How God Can and will restore your marriage" and I am

receiving the daily Encouragement ("My Beloved Daily Devotional"). I just want to know if God really wants my family together or not, since I am not legally married, but we have a young child together. I am so ready to follow the steps to obedience but since I am not in a situation of Marriage, how can I follow what He wants if at first He maybe did not want us to form a family?

When I got my evaluation back, the part they had highlighted explained something that was key, how I needed to think of my relationship in comparison to the other women who came who were married. It said:

***Keep in mind that you should think of your relationship as a **divorced** woman—since this omits some of the principles reserved for women would are legally married as His protection over you :) as your Heavenly Father betrothed to His Son, such as refraining from any further intimacy. Yet just about every other principle does relate to you—especially since you have a child together.

So, remember, as soon as your boyfriend's heart turns back to you, keep in mind what He wants for you, and refrain from any intimacy until you are legally married—thus giving you and your child a stable environment where you both will be able to thrive. Here is a RESTORED Marriage Testimony from *Sabrina in Georgia*, that will help encourage you.

Valerie do you have favorite Bible verses that you would like to pass on to women reading your Testimonies? Promises that He gave you?

"So do not fear, for I am with you; do not be dismayed, for I am your God. I will strengthen you and help you; I will uphold you with my righteous right hand." (Isaiah 41:10 - NIV)

"Give all your cares to the Lord and He will give you strength. He will never let those who are right with Him be shaken." (Psalm 55:22)

"Surely God does not reject one who is blameless or strengthen the hands of evildoers. He will yet fill your mouth with laughter and your lips with shouts of joy. Your enemies will be clothed in shame, and the tents of the wicked will be no more." (Job 8 20:22 - NIV)

"Instead of your shame you will receive a double portion, and instead of disgrace you will rejoice in your inheritance. And so you will inherit a double portion in your land, and everlasting joy will be yours." (Isaiah 61:7 - NIV)

Valerie would you be interested in helping encourage other women?

Yes. I am currently attending law school, but still having time to help with the French / Français translations as I began doing shortly after coming to RMI. I always wanted to help others but I did not know how and who to help. Also, lately I felt like I needed to improve my English so I see this as an opportunity to do both! :)

I have been raised a Christian and I always been a true believer. Since the beginning of this journey, I have learned to get closer to Him, make Him first in my life and understanding better His word (although I am still learning to do all that better).

Though I've always tithed, since I was part of the ministry team (who all tithe where they are spiritually fed), I knew that by forgetting to tithe it would have a bad consequences for everyone, fellow ministers and also on those who come here we hope to help.

Either way Valerie, what kind of encouragement would you like to leave women with, in conclusion?

Dear brides, although, I did fail AGAIN and again to follow the principles and to be His bride, He helped me start again and He will help you too. And although it hurt to have to restart from the beginning and to also deal with human rejection, I felt something more peaceful the second time I started over, something different ins me than the time I failed before. So my message is this, the more we get close to Him, even when we fall, we can experience peace!

Dear bride, don't let fear win. And do not try to do it your own way. The principles are accurate because they are from God.

~ *Valerie in New York, RESTORED*

Chapter 3

Envia

"Jesus said to him: 'Did not I say
that if you believed you would
see the glory of God?'"
—John 11:40

"This New Life is a Gift from God"

**What brought you to RMI? Please use this space to briefly let our
readers know what your life was like when you first found us, Envia, so
our readers understand just what a miracle your restoration is.**

Envia, how did your restoration actually begin?

In April 2016 my husband left home, resentful, bitter and determined to
never come back after 13 years of marriage. I started my struggle with the
Lord one month before he left, which helped me to understand, but not to
avoid the deep pain and heartbreaking situation.

My husband made this decision because I was not living as a Christian wife
should act. Most of the time I was contentious, quarrelsome, bossy, and
usurped the role of my husband as head of household. Besides that, the
worst sin that I committed, was to have made an idol of my husband and by
doing so, I removed God from our lives.

During this restoration journey many horrible and difficult things happened,
but in each one, without exception— the Lord stood beside me! He taught
me that every moment and every valley I went through was necessary. Then,
He and His great love and mercy would heal and restore my heart. Also,
due to being transparent about my shortcomings, my daughters and
especially my family were also healed during this journey.

At first the resource that helped me cope with the battle was the book *How
God Can and Will Restore Your Marriage*, which helped me completely
understand that the Lord had everything under His power and that He must

first change me. For all of you who still want restoration, you must put Him first, trust Him and no one else. Then believe what He promises and let Him make the changes in you. For me, this has been an indispensable process that allowed Him to restore me first, then our marriage.

How did God change your situation Envia as you sought Him wholeheartedly?

After a year of fighting, which only meant my husband hated me more, not to mention the great distance between us and zero chance of reconciliation, I received my first sign. The Lord began to work on my husband. This was after Him knowing that I was already completely His and my heart belonged to Him alone. My husband lost his excellent, well-paying job. As a result, he had no choice but to leave the luxury apartment where he lived. He was forced to return to where his parents lived. I, throughout that time, had always declared that staying in that place (his luxury apartment) was going to be temporary and so—God was faithful and pulled him away. He took him to live with his parents, where I had asked God to put him, to give us, my HH and me even more time to be together before restoration.

My husband's heart was hardened, despite the humiliating ordeal he was going through. For me, it seemed that was not what he might have prayed for me. My humiliation forced me to give my life to the Lord because I had to live one difficult thing after another difficult, very painful experience. I knew God was working on me, changing me and making me whole again, after sending me into the fire over and over again. God rearranged my heart so that his son was now first. This has been the secret of our Beloved Father, being able to work and change everything!

What principles, from God's Word (or through our resources), Envia, did the Lord teach you during this trial?

Being a wise, pure woman. To be the helpmate to my husband and a good mother to my daughters. To be a better person in my daily life and a good daughter to my parents and in-laws. To be a wise woman.

Tithing changed everything. Before I was willing to tithe and surrender and trust Him, due to fear, I saw no changes. Even after tithing, it didn't happen until I was resolved that I needed to give to my storehouse, here at RMI. This is when each of the resources began to come alive and I began to live in joy, love, and peace.

What were the most difficult times that God helped you through Envia?

Hatred and indifference from my husband, who acted as if I had never seen or known him before. He was someone I didn't know, no one my children wanted to be around. Everyone said he was different and to move on to find someone else, a better man.

Envia, what was the "turning point" of your restoration?

The turning point was when I decided to drop my husband definitely in the hands of the Lord. Many times I gave my husband to Him, but one day I said, "Lord I do not need anyone else to be happy! I promise to stay with You and not look for any man, ever. From now on, You're going to be my Husband, now and forever." God was good and faithful and He saw my HH and I starting to grow closer each day.

Tell us HOW it happened Envia? Did your husband just walk in the front door? Envia, did you suspect or could you tell you were close to being restored?

In August, my oldest daughter had to have an operation and it was an emergency. I knew it was something that God had allowed for good, for a purpose and I wasn't frightened or concerned because I'd experienced His love. During the days in the hospital, my husband and I were with her. We slept there and lived there together in total peacefulness. That weekend, I prayed with faith and humility to the Lord and told Him I did not want to spend one more weekend as a broken family. I was ready for our family to be restored. I told Him I wanted and was finally ready to spend the days when we returned home being a family again. Going through this I saw Him turn my heart to want His will, no longer my own. And so, because He is so good and wonderful, God gave me this— my new heart's desire.

After returning home, my husband started coming to the house every weekend to spend time with our daughters and me and no longer took them out to spend time as he had been doing. After a few months, he began to sleep in our house, not in our bed, but under the same roof. I saw the Lord work every day, although the evidence on coexistence, I have to say, was even tougher. Nevertheless, I decided to believe our Beloved Heavenly Father and declare that if He had brought my husband here, He would complete the good work in each of us.

I was no longer the woman who fought and demanded her way. I was, with the help of the Lord, my HH, a calm, wise and gentle spirit. In addition, my husband began to join in all our family prayers—he participated willingly (when previously wanting nothing, absolutely nothing of God)! He knew that our Father was in our home and that the peace he felt was there because He was our Father. I contemplated not praying as we'd done, but it was my daughters who insisted and initiated it each morning and evening.

In December, my husband, after a conversation he had with his parents, decided it was time to fully return and he announced it to our daughters. They became so happy, knowing that God had answered every prayer and that He had never been far from our suffering and pain.

On January 1st, the first day of the New Year, my husband began coming in and sleeping with me. Surprisingly (because I no longer needed it or wanted it), he apologized for leaving and said, "Let's leave the past behind and start over from scratch. Let's have a new marriage."

Restoration takes time, but day by day the Lord does His work. All that I went through was worth living. No, I'm still not the perfect woman and neither is my husband the perfect man. Now that we have the Lord in the middle of our lives, and we know that while living in our home (which will be forever), everything will work according to His perfect work—we do live a perfect life and restoration.

You could see that you suspected or were close to being restored?

Yes, I was fully aware. God gave me many, many signs that it would be restored despite the horrible circumstances. It's only because of the resources that I knew what to look for.

Would you recommend any of our resource in particular that helped you Envia?

How God Can and Will Restore Your Marriage and also *A Wise Woman*. Read *By the Word of Their Testimonies*. Find your HH by doing the *Finding the Abundant Life* Course. I am still going through online courses to keep my heart right and my mind focused on Him.

And also, everyone who has come here for help, be sure you faithfully share HopeAtLast.com with anyone you know is having marriage issues. I pull it up on their phone and then turn them over to God to finish the restoration process, watching Him change one life and heal one family after another.

Do you have favorite Bible verses you would like to share with women who read your testimony? Or promises he gave you?

Psalm 37:4 "Delight yourself in the LORD; And He will give you the desires of your heart. Commit your way to the LORD, Trust also in Him, and He will do it. And He will bring forth your righteousness as the light...Rest in the LORD and wait patiently for Him; Do not fret because of him who prospers in his way...Do not fret, it leads only to evildoing...But those who wait for the LORD, they will inherit the land."

2 Corinthians 10: 3-6 "O let the evil of the wicked come to an end, but establish the righteous. I shall not be afraid of evil tidings; my heart is fixed, trusting in the Lord. My heart is established; I shall not be afraid, until I see my desire come upon the enemy."

John 11:40 "Jesus said to him: 'Did not I say that if you believed you would see the glory of God?'"

Zechariah 9:12 "Return to the stronghold, you prisoners, with hope; today I declare that I will return double what was taken from you."

Ezekiel 36:26 "Moreover, I will give you a new heart and put a new spirit within you; I will remove from your body the heart of stone and give you a heart of flesh."

1 Peter 3 "Likewise, ye wives, be submissive to your husbands, so that if some of them are disobedient to the word, they may be won over without words by the behavior of their wives."

Isaiah 49:8 "Thus says the Lord: 'In an acceptable time I have answered you, in a day of salvation I have helped you; I will keep you and give you for a covenant of the people, to restore the earth to inherit the desolate heritages."

Psalm 1:1 "Blessed is the man who walks not in the counsel of the wicked or stands in the way of sinners, nor sits in the seat of scoffers, but His delight is in the law of the Lord and meditates on it day and night."

Would you be interested in helping encourage other women Envia?

Totally

Either way Envia, what kind of encouragement would you like to leave women with, in conclusion?

There is no reason not to believe the promises of the Lord. He said He can and will restore your marriage. But, it will not be along the easiest road. This is His way to ensure your full salvation and eternity next to Him and so you can find that abundant life we all need.

My husband and I are reliving all the good and living the new life that has been doing things the Lord's way and putting God first. This new life is a gift from God.

I decided to believe, obey and love God, and He was good and faithful to bring my family together again. I promise if you do the same, He will do the same with each of you. If you believe and are committed to pursuing the most wonderful Husband above all else—you will experience the most wonderful journey of your lives.

Chapter 4

Faith

"Now to Him who is able to do
immeasurably more than all
we ask or imagine"
—Ephesians 3:20

"More Than One Miracle"

It's been almost 5 years that I heard the words that no newly married woman wants to hear from her husband. One morning as my husband left for work he said, "Today during my lunch hour I'm going to find an attorney to file for divorce." Praise the Lord! My husband NEVER kept that appointment because that day I cried out to the Lord for Him to help and he sent a woman, an angel, to help me get through the scariest week of my life.

As soon as I got to church for my weekly bible study, I almost immediately ran into the ladies room and began sobbing. I was sitting on the couch in the lounge when I know God immediately heard my cry and sent a woman who saw me crying my heart out. She sat down and wrapped her arms around me and without even telling her why I was crying, she began to comforted me, telling me that everything would be okay and that my marriage would be fine, not to worry!!

Seeing me so pregnant anyone else would have thought it was my baby who I was crying about or me just being hormonal, but this women knew. Once I calmed down she reached into her bag and handed me the book How God Will Restore Your Marriage, then she took my hands and we prayed together. That very night my husband became violently ill. The very next morning my husband got ready for work, but when he left he said, "I won't be keeping the appointment with my attorney like I said." THANK GOD, God had turned my husband's heart just as the woman prayed would happen!

So I thought my miracle was complete but it actually had only begun. My trials were actually far from over. A month later I began to lose our first baby. I was rushed to the hospital after calling my doctor to let him know what was happening. One thing I need to mention, I was pregnant when my husband and I got married. We were going to the church and we'd met in the college and career group. Soon after meeting my husband and I began dating and I'm ashamed to say we didn't remain pure. When I realized I was pregnant, I told my parents because I didn't know what to do. My father had me call my boyfriend, and told him to sit down and then told him we would marry. So I knew my husband always felt he was made to marry me and I'm sure regretted being forced into it.

Though I was so scared I'd lose the baby and that my husband would be relieved he could just walk away from me, I also felt that it was my punishment for what I'd done. But God is so good, He had another reason for me almost losing our baby. While I was there in the hospital for those two weeks, my husband's attitude totally changed towards me. One night when they thought they couldn't get a heartbeat, my husband dropped to his knees by my bed and pleaded with God to save the life of our baby girl.

Only a few days later I went into labor, and praise God we received another miracle. Our little girl was just fine! She was a healthy baby and she weighed a full 7 lbs.—not the premature baby the doctors had said she'd be!

Six weeks later, together we stood together at the altar dedicating our precious baby girl to the Lord. And as we prayed I looked up to see the woman who'd prayed for me that day sitting near the front row. I could see there were tears streaming down her face as our eyes met. No one but the two of us knew there was more than one miracle to be thankful for!!

~ Faith in Australia, RESTORED

Chapter 5

Janice

"A broken and a contrite heart,
O God, You will not despise."
—Psalm 51:17

"She Had it All"

Everyone used to tell me I "had it all." I had a handsome husband who "worshiped" me, two beautiful sons, dozens of close friends and a brand-new home. But I was discontented with my life. I honestly did not appreciate what God had given me and as far as my devoted husband, I am ashamed to say that I would often comment to my friends when we'd get together, "I wish he would find someone else." What was I thinking and how could I ever have said anything so idiotic?!?!

After my two boys were in school the Lord saw past my horrible attitude and blessed me with a daughter, the most adorable baby girl I could ever have imagined. She had beautiful blue eyes and blonde hair like me. This event changed my life, but only slightly. I cherished this baby girl, but unfortunately my heart was still cold toward my husband. During any and all of our arguments, I would state emphatically, screaming, pointing at the door or holding it open, "Go ahead and leave - and don't let the door hit you on the way out!"

One horribly heated argument, which I later found out was my husband's breaking point, is when he said something that really set me off. I slapped him so hard that it knocked him backward and he landed on the floor. Looking back, the fact that he didn't get up and hit me or yell at me proved what a good man I had. Instead, he simply got up and walked out the door. Doing nothing more emphasized the truth about me as the horribly contentious woman that I was, but also even more about the wonderful man I had been blessed with.

Only when it was too late did I discover that God's Word says, "For by your words you shall be justified, and by your words, you shall be condemned" (Matthew 12:37). MY words would condemn me and break me into a million pieces. It happened one night that I was out with my friends. I came back earlier than we'd planned and when I walked into our bedroom, I found my husband in bed with another woman. This man who had adored me since we were in elementary school!! I stood shocked at the door and noticed that the other woman in his arms, in our bed, was one of our closest friends!!

All I can say is that the shock and incredible pain that hit me that day was more than I ever knew existed. I was so devastation and the shock was so great that for weeks I could only lay curled up in a fetal position, moaning and crying, completely unable to eat or speak to anyone. If not for many of my friends and my family who began coming in to help care for me and for my children, I don't know what I'd have done. My husband was gone, he left the moment I began screaming and collapsed on the bedroom floor in sobs with more blood-curdling screams that woke our children who witnessed what happened. I had no idea if he packed bags (later I discovered he did) nor did I ever see the OW leave.

It was then that the Lord took me, broken and beyond any reasoning, into Himself and began to hold me and comfort me, rocking me gently in His arms. After I came back to reality, though I was never the same person who walked into my bedroom that night, my mother came in one day, sat on my bed and reminded me about this woman, Erin, and her books and fellowship my mother attended. My mother tried to coax me to come with her many times before, but I couldn't stand "Erin." That's all my mom could talk about, what Erin said about this and that. So just like my attitude towards my husband, I used to tell everyone I hated her, when I knew nothing about her.

It's almost laughable now if it wasn't so pathetic, but Erin and I became very close friends. Because my mother had been going to her fellowship meetings (Erin actually told me my mom was one of the first women in her fellowship), Erin was willing to come to meet me before I was even able to get out of bed. While still recovering, I began reading her books and once I was able to get up, I began applying the principles I discovered in *How God Can and Will Restore Your Marriage* book after I had read *A Wise Woman* because this is the book my mom had begged me to read (she knew our marriage was in trouble). So, this was my first step towards restoration, honoring my mother, which I read was the first commandment with a promise.

After being gone for six months, with me making changes every day (by His grace and because of finding His love for me), my husband returned home—home to me and our three children—coming back to a new Janice. Soon after we were restored, we moved away, away from family, away from friends, and thankfully away from the many other OWs I'd heard he had been involved with during the six months of our separation. Though I didn't want to move, I was agreeable when my husband got a new job and approached me about moving with him, understanding that it was God giving us a fresh start in our new life together.

What I'd like to say in my testimony is to be a real friend. Please care enough to encourage your friends, all the women you know, to love your friends enough to force them to learn the truth before it's too late. Only God knows the damage I did to my husband and my marriage. And rather than my friends rallying around and forcing me to see who I really was and how I was destroying my life, they just laughed it off and said, "Oh, that's just Janice." Friends don't accept destructive behavior if they really care.

Thankfully most of how I used to be I can't remember any more. During my recovery, I prayed daily many prayers from Erin's book, one I prayed earnestly was that neither my husband or children would remember the old me or what happened that night or the state I was in afterward. In the RYM book it says: "Pray that God will forgive your transgressions and blot out the bad memories your husband has (Psalms 9:6) "The very memory of them has perished" and replace them with good thoughts. Pray harder and be sweeter (again, "sweetness of speech adds persuasiveness") at every opportunity that you may have with your husband to win him back. Remember, "A brother offended is harder to be won than a strong city, and contentions are like the bars of a castle" Proverbs 18:19.

Thankfully it wasn't too late for me to study "Won Without a Word" and especially the "Contentious Woman"—but please remember, it might be too late for one of your friends or a sister you love.

Please don't let them destroy themselves and the innocent children that are the victims of our crazy behavior as women.

~ *Janice in South Carolina, RESTORED*

Chapter 6

Vanessa

"Commit your way to the Lord,
Trust also in Him,
and He will do it."
—Psalm 37:5

"My Only Refuge"

Vanessa, how did your restoration actually begin?

I've been a Christian since I was little. My husband and I had been together for 7 years and he became the love of my life, my first boyfriend. After many months of arguments, setting my eyes on someone else and leaving my home for over two months, in search of my "dreams" in the show business, living in a friend's house, my husband fell in love with someone else due to my stubbornness.

Thanks to the prayers of my husband, family and friends; even despite my husband didn't love me anymore, God turned my heart and made me realize the grave mistake I was making. Repentant, I asked my husband for forgiveness and to allow me to come home and he did. Everything was fine the first few days, but I was still contentious, nagging him and filled with pride and the pain knowing he was in love with another woman would torment me. My relationship with God wasn't the best and I still harbored desires to continue my artistic career; something that I now know caused the slow detriment of my marriage.

Living together again, my husband told me he couldn't see me as a woman again, but like a sister and a friend, but not as a wife. This hurt me so much, and this was the point in which God placed in my heart a desire to seek Him if I wanted my marriage to be restored. I had already asked the Lord for forgiveness but I was unable to forgive myself, regret tormented me.

Desperate, I started searching for restored marriage testimonies online, praying to God for direction to find the right resource. I found Restore Ministries and the book *How God Can and Will Restore Your Marriage*. That's when I started to read the Bible with a passion, my soul was shattered, and I cried, feeling desolated, feeling that if my husband didn't love me again I would die.

But I didn't give up, I kept reading the RYM book, and then God showed me that I needed to focus in my relationship with Him, my HH. The first few weeks were hard because I kept pursuing my husband and he kept rejecting me. I found a prayer partner when I asked God for one. I also decided to fast half a day.

I went back to church after many years and was given the privilege of serving in the worship ministry. It was at that point where things started to intensify and me and my husband decided to sleep separately. Those were hard days. My heart was hurting and I cried a lot. Doubt crept into my mind and I wanted to quit and fly to a different state, to my aunt and uncle's house. But God didn't let that happen, He kept me standing through the trial with my heart focused on Him. I kept praying, reading, fasting, seeking God's Word before anything else.

At the beginning I made the mistake of telling everyone about my situation, seeking refuge and help. It wasn't until I understood that God was my only refuge that I turned to Him. Then on a Saturday, when I fasted the entire day, I asked Him to remove this affliction and that I wanted to see Him as my only Source of peace and joy, my only Refuge, my Father, my HH, my Friend.

That afternoon was the last time I cried from pain. My HH gave me the opportunity to bless a friend who was going through something similar, with a broken heart and gravely ill in the hospital. God brought His Word to her life through me, I prayed for her and after that, God restored an incomprehensible peace within my heart. Though my mind knew I was having problems, my spirit was at peace. From there on His peace has not left me and I asked my HH to remain in me. From that day forward my relationship with my HH became closer than ever and I started to know my God of the impossible.

Things at home were in bad shape, I still slept in a different room from my husband. I prayed that if it was His will my husband would ask me to get back together. I felt that was impossible because my husband had so much pride and always kept telling me that he couldn't forget what I'd done. He had forgiven me but he couldn't forget it. As I continued praying, I found a book that told about the importance of praying for our husbands and to turn to God with our requests instead of complaining to them.

I finished reading the *Restore Your Marriage* book and found the resource of taking the courses and it was there where I found more testimonies that I could study. I spoke with my pastors and they told me not to give up and to fight for my home. A beloved aunt of mine and who is one of my teachers of faith since childhood, prayed for me and prophesied about my life and my husband's life. She told me that God was going to use us both to minister and to restore marriages, and to minister to youth and instruct them towards a good future marriage. Even after this beautiful promise from God, fear and doubt crept in, but I always asked God to forgive me and to help me overcome it. I've always asked Him for the Holy Spirit to guide me and give me the victory in Him.

To God be the glory, and to my surprise, God allowed my husband to seek me out on Thursday morning when he came to ask me to sleep with him, something he'd always denied me. He hugged me and asked me for forgiveness, and told me he loved me. I couldn't believe it, I thanked God and cried from happiness. My husband made a commitment with me and said that I could be at ease for he'd be with me to respect me.

It hurts that my husband's heart is still in pain as he confessed his fear to me when he gave me his heart again; he's afraid of going through this again. But at the same time, he told me not to worry, that we can get through this with God's help. I know there's still things to change in each of us, and that maybe attacks from the enemy will get worse, but I'm not afraid because God is with us. I don't think I'll ignore any open doors to get my blessing stolen again. HE is the center of my life and my help.

Also, I want to keep going with my courses because my longing is to be an instrument in God's hands to bless other families. This world is being destroyed through family disintegration; bad advisors and therapists are accelerating separations instead of repairing or restoring. I'm convinced that the only One Who restores is my God, it's HIM, our HH.

My dear brother or sister, don't give up, when the storm gets stronger, then your miracle is just around the corner. Continue holding onto your HH hand and turn your faith and life over to Him.

Now I know that God allowed this to open my eyes and show me His perfect bidding. I argued a lot and wouldn't accept the biblical commandment that women have to submit to their husbands, I was a feminist. I said I loved God but how could that be when I didn't obey His commandments? But glory be to God because He opened my eyes and told me His order, the Lord is the head of my husband, my husband is my authority and I am his helpmeet.

Fight for the treasure of your life's most precious ministry, your family by turning your heart to your HH. The enemy is always striving to tempt us and destroy our homes, because he knows that he won't be only destroying the couple but also the children, family members and friends. God wants you to be certain that He wants to restore your marriage. He wants us to be whole in Him. Families are a representation of His kingdom.

Let's carry on firmly towards our goal. If God is for us who can be against us?

How did God change your situation Vanessa as you sought Him wholeheartedly?

The change was instant. His peace was restored in my heart the instant I decided to rest in His hands completely. When I stopped pursuing and controlling my husband. When I stopped wanting to fix things by myself. I want to live like this forever. I love You my HH.

What principles, from God's Word (or through our resources), Vanessa, did the Lord teach you during this trial?

He must be first in our lives.

The importance of seeing the trunk in our eyes instead of the straw in the other person.

To serve His kingdom.

The order of the home, the authority that God has given our husbands over us women.

To pray when something bothers, to present my cause before God, instead of seeking other people.

Prayer is more effective than a thousand complaints or words to the one who offends.

To forgive and to be forgiven.

Nothing is impossible to God.

What were the most difficult times that God helped you through Vanessa?

I felt completely alone. In this country, I have my husband's support and his family. My immediate family is in my country of origin and I have relatives that support me but they live in a different state. The more alone, abandoned and unworthy I felt, He picked me up with His love and filled me with peace.

Vanessa, what was the "turning point" of your restoration?

Turning my life completely to God and seeking to obey Him. That was a decisive moment for the change in my life.

To use the tools God left us for spiritual warfare, because it is not against flesh but against principalities and powers. Prayer, His Word, fasting. The power to bind and untie was given to us through God's Son.

Tell us HOW it happened Vanessa? Did your husband just walk in the front door?

My husband called me and asked me to return to our bedroom. We were living together but our hearts and bedrooms were apart. Curiously, ever since I started to pray for him, he started to get tense and uneasy. I think this was the Holy Spirit telling him the correct thing to do was to forgive me and fight for this. There was a big oppression of pride and belief of one's judgement, a wrong idea of forgiveness, that I know God wants to work with in his life now that He's got my heart.

Vanessa, did you suspect or could you tell you were close to being restored?

No, on the contrary, I was afraid this would take months to work out. My case is peculiar being that generally is the man who fails, in this case it was me. But against all odds, God is continually restoring. There were people who said they'd change their mind about God if we fixed our situation. I think this will be a great testimony that will change not only our lives but that of many.

Would you recommend any of our resource in particular that helped you Vanessa?

Of course I would. These resources have been a miracle from God to my life. Undoubtedly God made this project spring out of Erin's heart.

Do you have favorite Bible verses Vanessa that you would like to pass on to women reading your Testimonies? Promises that He gave you?

"Commit your way to the Lord, Trust also in Him, and He will do it." Psalm 37:5

"For the eyes of the Lord move to and fro throughout the earth that He may strongly support those whose heart is completely His." 2 Chronicles 16:9

"Then you will call, and the Lord will answer; you will cry, and He will say, 'here I am.' If you remove the yoke from your midst, the pointing of finger and speaking wickedness." Isaiah 58:9

"Then He said to me, "Do not be afraid, Daniel, for from the first day that you set your heart on understanding this and on humbling yourself before your God, your words were heard, and I have come in response to your words. But the king of the kingdom of Persia was withstanding me for twenty-one days..." Daniel 10:12–13.

"All the paths of the Lord are lovingkindness and truth to those who keep His covenant and His testimonies. For Your name's sake, o Lord, pardon my iniquity, for it is great. Who is the man who fears the Lord? He will instruct him in the way he should choose. His soul will abide in prosperity, and his descendants will inherit the land. The secret of the Lord is for those who fear Him, and He will make them know His covenant. My eyes are continually toward the Lord, for He will pluck my feet out of the net" Psalm 25:10–15.

"A constant dripping on a day of steady rain and a contentious woman are alike; he who would restrain her restrains the wind, and grasps oil with his right hand." Proverbs 27:15-16

"Many seek the ruler's favor, but justice for man comes from the Lord." Proverbs 29:26

"There is no wisdom and no understanding and no counsel against the Lord. The horse is prepared for the day of battle, but victory belongs to the Lord." Proverbs 21:30-01

Would you be interested in helping encourage other women Vanessa?

Yes

Either way, Vanessa, what kind of encouragement would you like to leave women with, in conclusion?

Do not fear, though it doesn't seem like it and you feel alone, God is holding your hand and has complete control over your situation. He's always on time. He allows us to go through the desert because it's the only way in which we'll turn to Him completely and know Him in ways we couldn't have imagined. God wants to prepare you to be a blessing to others.

~ Vanessa in Arizona

Chapter 7

Ivana

"But in my distress I cried out
to the Lord; yes, I prayed to my
God for help. He heard me from
His sanctuary; my cry to
Him reached His ears"
—Psalm 18:6

"True and Intimate Friend"

I am a wife who is living in RESTORED marriage, for 4 months already. We have three beautiful daughters.

We separated in July, because I had suspicions that my husband was unfaithful to me and became to treat me and our daughters differently. Then three months later I found the RMI website. I started to pray from the bottom of my heart for marriage restoration and I am so thankful to the Lord for answering my prayers and saving me. I immediately started to read your resources and also prayed for healing of my family. I started fasting too.

My husband returned home half a year later, it was right before Christmas. We really had blessed Christmas time together. First I was afraid if I did not let him in too early, but now I see, it was the Lord leading me and helping me to accept him back. My husband started to change - slowly but obviously. The Lord is so faithful and He is working on my marriage. I can see he is treating me nicer, he respects me more, he is spending more time with the kids. We even went to church together, as this never happened before. He is also coming back from work on time and is not working weekends.

I am so thankful to Jesus and also to this ministry. I bought three books for women, *How God Can and Will Restore Your Marriage*, *My Beloved*, and *A Wise Woman*. I also purchased three of the men's books, *How God Will*

Restore your Marriage, *A Wise Man*, and *My Beloved* and I am trying to live out all these principles.

I also started to tithe faithfully. I see such a blessing in tithing and this principle is also the one which I am trying to spread around for others to see the importance of tithing.

I am trying to submit to my husband so the Word of the Lord will not be dishonored. I am also trying to teach my daughters based on the teaching of a Wise Woman.

I want to encourage others that the same way how the Lord worked in my marriage, He will work in yours. If you have a problem, seek the Lord for answers in His Word.

Even though my husband is home, I believe only the Lord is the true and intimate Friend, Lover and He is the One who helped me in the most difficult time of my life. And He is always at hand.

~ Ivana in Slovakia, RESTORED

Chapter 8

Gail

"My blessing is on those people
who trust in me, who put
their confidence in me."
—Jeremiah 17:7

"Made My Restoration Solid"

Gail, how did your restoration actually begin?

I found your website through another website when I was looking for someone who had results of a restored marriage. I was married with two kids, and my husband and I were physically separated because of his work and not by choice.

Everything was always good, we were chatting and emailing each other regularly. Our problem started because I was always checking on him. One day he just said he cannot do it anymore and said he won't come home anymore during his vacation. He slowly became cold and distant. That's when I discovered a lot of things and someone tried to tell me he was having an affair and told me her name but when I asked him, he said it was not true and I believed him, but he was really different.

We continued our usual communication but it was not the same. He would always find excuses not to chat with me and the kids. Then I discovered everything and I tried to contact the girl he was involved with through FB, my husband got upset and our problem became bigger. He became even more distant until he no longer called or messaged us anymore. I kept pursuing him like my FB group said to do. One day I called and it was the girl who answered.

How did God change your situation Gail as you sought Him wholeheartedly?

It was tough, but after finding RMI, I turned everything over to God and let go. Only a month later his company transferred him praise God so he was no longer working with the girl.

I first learned that God heals all hurts and bitterness by taking the courses. Then, I learned to forgive my husband completely. When I became gentle and kind to him, he began to see the difference in the way I talked to him and that made him want to come home when he had vacation time.

What principles, from God's Word (or through our resources), Gail, did the Lord teach you during this trial?

I learned to stayed away and never contacted him. Before learning this, I always pursued him, always thought about him, always talked about him. But once my HH became first, that's when my EH began calling and pursuing me, and as I watched his heart turn back to me and our children I was in awe at how everything RMI says is true.

I learned, too, that I had to stand on God's Word, especially when my husband didn't give us any chance for restoration. He had totally given up on us. The Lord blessed me with two women to help me believe when I became weary. I asked God for an ePartner, a woman I could encourage who was going through a marriage crisis. Instead of finding just one ePartner, God gave me two!!! I shared the resources with them, even purchased books for them both.

To encourage myself, I would go to your website and read the testimonies of marriages restored and then I would tell my ePartners (they didn't have internet access) and it would actually encourage me. We would discuss what the restored wives did and set our hearts to do the same.

Gail, what was the "turning point" of your restoration?

For sure it was focusing on my HH and second was encouraging other women. Finding my ePartners was what turned my journey to become enjoyable. Before that I wasn't able to enjoy any part of my life. I struggled with everything.

To all the women who do not know what to do, the courses will help you get through the toughest of times, especially when you want to give up. Once you get to FAL, you will know you have a HH who has the love you've been longing for. You will little by little change to a better and more Godly woman and wife the more you give Him your heart.

What were the most difficult times that God helped you through Gail?

Letting go, deactivating my FB and then shifting my heart from my EH to my HH where it needed to be all along. I declared that one day I would be writing my testimony and here I am!

Without my HH I don't know where I would be. It became the toughest when I knew everything about my EH and the OW. My insecurities were being fed each time my EH confessed his true feelings and plans to be with the OW. Yet, spiritually I knew his plans didn't matter and as long as I focused my attention on my HH who is always faithful, I was able to forgive and love and encourage other women.

I truly thank the Lord because He has been faithful to do what His Word says He would do. Not only that, but others around me have the opportunity to witness what the Lord did for us. It was long time, but the Lord kept giving me His Word, reminding me these weren't just words to hope for, but promises He gave to me. So as long as I was faithful to Him, He would be faithful to me.

Tell us HOW it happened Gail? Did your husband just walk in the front door?

Late one night my husband had a big fight with the OW. He packed his things, left her house, and moved in with a friend, but his friend's wife did not want him there. He had no other place to go. So, he called me a day later, quit his job, and came home after living out of state with the OW.

He was broken, but the "Wise Woman workbook" had prepared me for his return. Things were shaky in the beginning. I had learn to listen to the Holy Spirit telling me not to say anything about the things he does that I didn't like, and to allow Him to complete the work He began in my husband. Praise the Lord, though it was tough, the more I fell in love with my HH the more my husband began to change!

Gail, did you suspect or could you tell you were close to being restored?

Yes and no. No because things were in the natural getting worse and worse. Everyone was telling me to give up, and I agreed, but in my heart I would give it to God, and then get closer to my HH That's when I saw things through His eyes. It's something I read several times in the resources, that when things are getting worse, you're so close. So this is why I could tell I was close, but that scared me because I knew things would become even harder.

Do you have favorite Bible verses Gail that you would like to pass on to women reading your Testimonies? Promises that He gave you?

Jeremiah 29:11-14 NET Bible "For I know what I have planned for you,' says the Lord. 'I have plans to prosper you, not to harm you. I have plans to give you a future filled with hope. When you call out to me and come to me in prayer, I will hear your prayers. When you seek me in prayer and worship, you will find me available to you. If you seek me with all your heart and soul, I will make myself available to you,' says the Lord. 'Then I will reverse your plight and will regather you from all the nations and all the places where I have exiled you,' says the Lord. 'I will bring you back to the place from which I exiled you.'"

Jeremiah 17:7 NET Bible "My blessing is on those people who trust in me, who put their confidence in me."

Would you recommend any of our resource in particular that helped you Gail?

The first resource I purchased was *How God Can and Will Restore Your Marriage* and *A Wise Woman*. I ordered copies for one friend and my brother, too. I wholeheartedly recommend both resources to encourage every woman and man in their walk as a believer.

Later I began to purchase the books by the case (more women's then men's) so I always had them to hand out. Now when I am able to share what God did for me, more women want the book.

Would you be interested in helping encourage other women Gail?

YES. I think to maintain restoration everyone needs to focus on helping others. It not only keeps God on your side, but it also keeps your focus on others and not on yourself. I also find that if I'm not involved this way, I tend to want to make sure I am "pleasing" to my husband when it's by pleasing the Lord, my HH, that makes my restored marriage solid.

Either way Gail, what kind of encouragement would you like to leave women with, in conclusion?

Dear Brides, we all want lives of abundance don't we, living free of worrying. Here is what I would encourage you to do. Every time you surrender and give up yourself and focus on loving HIM, the more of His *Abundant Life* you will find and the more you will want of Him.

All you need and all you should want to love for is Him and once you feel this way, He will take care of everything else because He wants to be your Everything!!! The enemy is keen to steal kill and destroy, but our HH said that He will come to you not to judge you but so that you can have a life of abundance. It's much more than having your marriage restored, it's living a life that overflows.

An Abundant life is being secure that HE will provide each of us all we need and most of what we want. It may not be the material stuff but what's most important to us as women—an abundance of love and the joy unspeakable and peace that surpasses all understanding. Keep on pressing toward your HH because only then will you find and experience the abundant life with Him when He gives you the desires of your heart. If you want someone who will never leave you or turn away from you, it is Him.

~ Gail in New York

Chapter 9

Laura

"He is before all things,
and in Him all things
hold together."
—Colossians 1:17

"What a Gift!"

First, I just want to say Praise God! He is so faithful to His promises!! My story is like so many others. I was devastated when my husband called after work one day and said he wasn't coming home. I knew that our marriage wasn't great, but I never dreamed that things would go that far. I later found out that my husband had been unfaithful to me for many months.

It was after he had been gone a week that someone recommended me to Restore Ministries. I cried and cried as I read the opening page of the website. Finally, here was some hope! I ordered the book *How God Can and Will Restore Your Marriage, A Wise Woman* workbook and joined the fellowship right away. I was shocked at how much I didn't know what God and what His Word had to say about marriage, divorce, and separation. But after reading everything, I knew that God would restore my marriage.

I began applying the principles right away. Although I didn't see immediate changes in my husband, I felt such peace like I had not felt in years. After my husband had been gone about three weeks, I re-dedicated my life to the Lord, and for what I believe is the first time in my life, I had an assurance of my salvation. What a gift!!

That's when the Lord became my everything, so much so that I really came to the place that I didn't even care if my marriage was ever restored. I no longer was waiting for my husband to call or come by, and if he did, I realized he would find out my feelings for him were actually sort of "indifferent." I didn't know it at the time, but that got my husband's attention.

Early on, right after he left, I had tried to act like I didn't care, my way of letting go, but he could see right through me. I was trying to act like I didn't care, but later when I really no longer cared for him that's when he noticed. It wasn't until I found my new LOVE, the Lord!! Becoming His bride was nothing anyone ever taught me, not in any of the churches or bible studies I'd attended over the many years I believed myself to be a Christian. It took my marriage falling apart for me to first find the assurance of my salvation (which I probably never had because I didn't really know Him personally like I do now), and also finding a love that heals.

There are many things in my past that happened to me and things I did to deaden the pain and shame I felt. Nothing ever helped me feel clean and worthy until He was truly my HH. That's when everything happened and my life began to change.

My marriage restoration happened one morning after my husband had been gone for almost two months. I got a phone call from my husband who called me from work and told me that his living arrangements were changing. I just said "ok" because I was no longer desperate and actually I wasn't really interested in what he was doing. That's the moment my husband actually began to weep and told me that he missed me, missed his family, his home, and the life he had. He wanted to try and get it all back. My HH is so amazing!! Had I not heard my EH break down, I don't believe I would have felt my heart change and turn back to him! I knew my husband needed more than just us back together or the life he had to be happy. He needed the Love that changed me!

What's crazy is that this was only 10 days after he came by to talk about how we were going to divide up everything in our house, about child visitation with our two boys, and about how I needed to figure out a way to support myself!!! He was so cold and heartless but it didn't bother me at all. I just had no feelings whatsoever for him and I found out later he could sense that was how I felt. I had my HH and I was actually restored. Who could ever have imagined such a drastic change in me.

It's so true that when we fully let go, and the Lord becomes our everything, our HH, that God will move. Also that it's okay to no longer want our marriages restored, as long as it's because we have so much of Him. God turned my heart so that my husband would see and feel that none of what he was saying mattered to me! It caused him to want us back and that's when God was able to move on our family's behalf.

That very next Sunday we went to church as a family for the first time ever. Then during the song at the end, when the invitation was given, I looked at my husband. He'd suddenly just collapsed down in his seat with his eyes closed and I could see tears were streaming down his face!!! A man in the front came down and asked him to come with him so he could pray for him. Ladies the Man who needs to be first in your life is the Lord. I wasn't even sure of my own salvation but once I came to know Him as my everything, He gave me everything! My husband has changed completely because I was willing to let go and give the Lord my complete life as His Bride.

Dear Bride, If not for your own sake, do it for your husband (or ex) who may also be trapped in sin like mine was. I never knew my husband was unfaithful, though I should have. But it is what God needed to happen for all of this to happen. I am just so grateful!!!

~ *Laura in Tennessee, RESTORED*

Chapter 10

Emily

"The mind of man
plans his way, but the
Lord directs his steps."
—Proverbs 16:9

"He Changed Me, Restored Me and Blessed Us with Our Daughter"

What brought you to RMI? Please use this space to briefly let our readers know what your life was like when you first found us, Emily, so our readers understand just what a miracle your restoration is.

Emily, how did your restoration actually begin?

My marriage was in crisis long before I realized it. We were a young couple, very happy, and we both had a dream of having a child. But when I got pregnant, things got complicated. Because I was never a woman as God teaches us in His Word and asks us to be as a wife, my world began to unravel.

From the time I was young, I always did what I thought was right. Like all of my friends, I was very manipulated by the media, wanting to be the independent, modern woman, which only led to utter failure of my marriage with heartbreaking results.

Only one month after our first child was born, my husband left home. Without a doubt, it was the worst blow I could have experienced as a first-time mother!

Saying I suffered a lot can't describe what I went through. Then, just when I thought it was the end, after spending awful nights, wishing to die because my husband said that he did not love me anymore and there was no hope for us, and that he wanted to live his life—God rescued me!

I was unable to simply move on like everyone said I should do. Honestly, I even tried. I went out with friends, but in my heart, my HH whispered, telling me "There was another way. This is not the end of your marriage."

How did God change your situation Emily as you sought Him wholeheartedly?

One night after my Heavenly Love touched my heart, I resolved to forgive my husband. I accepted the situation and took full responsibility for how my marriage had ended. I appointed a time to spend time with Him while my son slept.

Unfortunately, temptation got a hold of me. Instead of time with my HH, I would go out with my friends, in a desperate attempt to make my EH jealous. One day after I arrived at his house thinking I would find a happy man, which would strengthen me to stay on the path I'd rather follow. Just accept being separated and enjoy a new life with someone else.

Proverbs 16:9—
"The mind of man plans his way, but the Lord directs his steps."

Jeremiah 29:11—
"'For I know the plans that I have for you,' declares the LORD, 'plans for welfare and not for calamity to give you a future and a hope.'"

Isaiah 55:8–9—
"'For My thoughts are not your thoughts, neither are your ways My ways,' declares the Lord. 'For as the heavens are higher than the earth, so are My ways higher than your ways, and My thoughts than your thoughts.'"

His plan, what the Lord did, was to lead me along a path to shake me and take me where He wanted me to be, where He wanted me to go. When I went to leave my son with my EH, I saw my husband torn apart, moved to tears when he saw our son, and with the sweetest most tender look in his eyes.

After I left and went to join my friends, I was beyond devastated, and instead of enjoying myself, I began wondering—this could not possibly be the life that God wanted for us. I realized that there has to be another possibility, that our God had to do something to save us.

Rather than stay out, I left my friends and went home. I cried my heart out to the Lord begging Him to show me something, anything to help the mess I was in.

The next day I went to church, it was a Sunday, but I found no peace, no answers there. So I kept asking God to help me. Two days later, I'll never forget, it was on Tuesday when God showed me this wonderful Ministry. I was lost in the middle of a horrible desert, but the moment I found this ministry all hope returned! I remember well the joy I felt when I began to read the book *How God Can and Will Restore Your Marriage*. And that's where the most wonderful experience happened, when my life with my HH first began, and my world, why I was alive all began to make sense again.

What principles, from God's Word (or through our resources), Emily, did the Lord teach you during this trial?

After reading the RYM book, I felt God begin to change me, little by little, He began opening my eyes. I immediately began to see my mistakes, and I was able to forgive my husband. I told him I forgave him and then asked him for forgiveness for all my faults that God had shown me. Even though he did not believe or accept what I said, I did what I thought He was telling me to do out of simple obedience with no expectations. The experience was magnificent.

Yet my husband insisted on a divorce, but God had already given me His promise. So, his insistence did not shake me. I learned more as I went through the courses, so I never confronted him again about anything. Instead, I said I trusted him, I stopped arguing with him about filing for divorce or money. All of this caused great changes in our relationship, even though he didn't say so. Yet, nothing more was brought up about divorce once I agreed, which really encouraged me.

Another principle that changed me a lot was to become the woman God asks us to be: gentle, quiet and submissive, to be the crown of our husbands. I no longer tore my house down, but instead because I was His bride and (my husband told me later) this is when I began to glow.

What were the most difficult times that God helped you through Emily?

There were many times that I found myself in despair before I trusted my HH. But honestly after I put my trust in Him, once I became His bride and He was truly my HH, everything seemed easier! My journey was light and things that would normally hurt me deeply, only left me momentarily saddened. I had my dear HH to comfort me so I stopped dreading or fearing anything.

Emily, what was the "turning point" of your restoration?

The turning point of my restoration was when I truly let my husband go, let him go in order for us to be free. It was actually easy once my HH was first in my life and in my heart. I no longer needed my EH to satisfy my needs, I did not need him for anything. I also no longer needed to question him about another woman, because it didn't matter anymore. I had my Lover and He always attended to me and my needs. When we saw each other, I always asked my Lord to give me a state of calm, to make me look beautiful for Him as His bride and so my Love calmed my heart.

Tell us HOW it happened Emily? Did your husband just walk in the front door? Emily, did you suspect or could you tell you were close to being restored?

My restoration was gradual, beginning when I forgave my EH and began to treat him with the respect and love I got from my HH. Each time I changed and became closer to my HH, my EH came closer to me.

Yet as so many other restored women have said, often when my EH would move closer, the next moment he'd disappear, then he'd reappear suddenly. Yet each time I would ask the Lord the same thing, let me be closer to Him. He was who was taking care of me, taking care of all of us.

There were times when we got very close to being restored, once at a friend's party. But just as quickly, he'd begin backing off and disappearing again and again. But because I was so close to the Lord, I never once despaired like I thought I would. Instead, I'd be thankful for more time alone with Him.

Then one day it happened. He approached again when I saw him at a friend's house but this time he made a plan. Mother's Day was the following week so he asked if he could take me to lunch, and it ended up we were together all that day. Then, during the following week, he started talking about buying a house and each time he talked of plans for us to live together again.

On the following Sunday, just one day before completing 9 months of being separated, we went to see some houses. When we returned, he did not say anything. That night he called and wanted to take me to church the following morning. On the way, we spoke of our favorite house and I noticed how he started to look at me. We were seen together, at church, and later on the way home, he said we would have to have a talk.

The next day my HH prepared me. We had our talk as planned, which was when he confessed some things I was unaware of. He broke down and asked me for forgiveness. And by the Lord's grace and His glory, our marriage was restored that day. I forgave him and it's when (he says) he fell in love with me all over again.

Today after being restored for more than three years. Our lives are based on the ways I've learned here at RMI. RMI has changed everything. It's impossible to believe that only a short time ago, I was introduced to and fell in love with my Beloved Lord, my HH, who did not leave me for a second during my journey. A journey that started out in such desperation and pain but soon turned to joy and elation. I met a Man who showed me a way through the desert and deep valleys, who fulfilled His every promise and whose Word changed my life. He changed me, restored me and then blessed me with my heart's desire—being able to conceive—giving us our baby daughter, Bella.

Having a Husband who is wonderful and caring means there is nothing too difficult or impossible for us to go through. He changes any situation when we just believe and trust Him. He will show you a way through and will do what only He can do for you.

Thank you, my Lord, my Husband, for being with me, for giving me the strength to pass through this desert so that I could know You as closely as I do. All honor and all glory to Your Name my Love.

Would you recommend any of our resource in particular that helped you Emily?

How God Can and Will Restore Your Marriage book alone, and finding your HH, while focusing on His every word, the word of God, will draw you closer to the only truth that exists along with a restored marriage.

Would you be interested in helping encourage other women Emily?

Yes

Either way Emily, what kind of encouragement would you like to leave women with, in conclusion?

Do not give up, whatever your situation, no matter how hopeless it looks and no matter how painful it gets, just don't give up. You must rely on the One who makes all the things impossible to happen. He changes everything. Just believe God can do it, and fall in love with your HH. Simply use what this ministry gives you because if you are here, it was God who sent you, and He has something wonderful for you.

Chapter 11

Sara

"A broken and a contrite heart,
O God, You will not despise."
—Psalm 51:17

"Restored Marriage After Cancer"

Sara how did your restoration actually begin?

I was looking desperately for information about how to make my husband return home after I made him leave (I was the one who told him to), after reading a lot of information (mainly psychological content that did not help me at all :(

The Lord guided me to look for marriage restoration websites. PTL, I found the RYM ministries and even though I had many doubts at the beginning, I started walking in my RJ holding my Beloved's hand as His bride. First, I got my health restoration (I had cancer and He helped me go through my chemo radiantly!) Then he helped me restore my finances and then most recently my marriage.

I need to say that I was seeking only for my marriage restoration when I started my RJ (because honestly my husband gone was the only thing that occupied my mind!). What I didn't know then, was that He restores EVERYTHING once we understand that His will is to go beyond the marriage to bring us closer to Him. And as I have read in many testimonies, restoration of your marriage comes when you already have given Him the place He deserves in your heart.

How did God change your situation, Sara, as you sought Him wholeheartedly?

He started to renew my mind and change my heart. He transformed me into a woman with a gentle and quiet spirit. He moved me to seek Him every day and to also make sure I also encourage other women along my Journey. I can honestly say that I'm a new person, woman and wife. I can't even recognize today the person I could be in the past and pray the Lord, so He guards me and helps me follow His commandments for the rest of my life.

God changes everything, He makes things new, but you never imagine to what extent and how serious He is about this once you start receiving His glorious and precious love!

What principles, from God's Word (or through our resources), did the Lord teach you during this trial Sara?

• To make Him first in my heart.

• To read His word every day.

• To claim His promises for my life.

• To submit to my EH.

• To let go of my EH and my church.

• To submit to all authority.

• To tithe.

• To follow His commandments.

Sara what were the most difficult times that God helped you get through during your Journey?

I can say that the most difficult time was to see my husband so distant and so confident about leaving me. I felt guilty, desperate and felt like there was no solution for my situation. My EH used to say that only a MIRACLE could put us together and that's exactly what He did. All glory to Him for changing my situation in such an amazing way!!!!

He's still helping me, as I'm adapting to my marriage again. He leads me to be quiet when is necessary, to pray and cry to Him when I'm not in agreement or when my EH is wrong. Also, He's helped me let go of my church that changed so many things in my life. That's when He gave me a group of hurting women to minister. He's also given me the chance to be healthy and to take care of myself more physically. He's restored my past relationships and has guided me to abandon some friendships that are not recommendable.

Sara what was the "turning point" of your restoration?

My EH started to see that I had changed, not because I could change, but because He is transforming me into the bride He wants. My EH acknowledged my change and started to consider the possibility for a future together again in spite of the many problems we had experienced in the past.

In addition to this, he started to make plans with me about the future, about how to renovate the house and also started to take more care of me and my daughter. Once he saw that I had a different attitude, he started to believe that things could be different. What he didn't know then is that I wasn't only "different"—I was in love—with the Love of my life, who made me His bride.

Tell us HOW it happened Sara? Did your husband just walk in the front door?

My HH confirmed to me that my marriage was already restored some time ago! My EH has some clothes at his parents, so I thought that I couldn't say our marriage was restored yet. But after praying for some time, He let me know that "His ways are higher than my ways" and that He chooses how restoration and the husband's return happens.

My EH lives with me, at home now, we make plans and decisions together and have even talked about another baby. HOW AMAZING!!! Because in the past this blessing was never on the table due to the many fights and problems we faced. I understand the Lord orchestrates everything in His perfect will and He will complete what He started. He's never late, always on time!!!

Did you suspect or could you tell you were close to being restored, Sara?

Yes, I could feel my restoration was close, because my EH spent more time with me and at home, and because I was not seeking for the marriage restoration anymore. I was IN LOVE with the best One ever and I knew in my heart that my HH would complete His works in my life soon. Also, my best friend and sister confirmed this to me. They felt my life wouldn't be restored in some aspects, but in every aspect!

Sara, would you recommend any of our resource in particular that helped you?

The *How God Can and Will Restore Your Marriage* Book, The Encourager, and the RRR online courses. They are a huge blessing and a necessary guide to understanding the Scripture's principles and the Lord's will for our lives. THANK YOU for these!!

Sara do you have favorite Bible verses that you would like to pass on to women reading your Testimonies? Promises that He gave you?

Philippians 4:19
And my God will meet all your needs according to the riches of his glory in Christ Jesus.

Proverbs 21:1
In the Lord's hand the king's heart is a stream of water that he channels toward all who please Him.

Psalm 112:7
They will have no fear of bad news; their hearts are steadfast, trusting in the Lord.

2 Corinthians 13:11
Rejoice! Strive for full restoration, encourage one another, be of one mind, live in peace. And the God of love and peace will be with you.

Sara, would you be interested in helping encourage other women?

Yes! I've joined the Spanish Team as a Translator which has been a dream of mine.

Either way, what kind of encouragement would you like to leave women with, in conclusion, Sara?

Trust God with all your heart, have conversations with Him only during the day, don't talk to anyone before talking to Him. Pray, fast, look for His word for you. Don't dismay, He sees your tears and is willing to help you cross the line of this RJ. Read the materials from Encouraging Bookstore and go through the free courses RMI offers and ask the Lord how you can succeed in this and begin helping.

~ Sara in Colón

Chapter 12

Raquel

"For His anger is but for a moment,
His favor is for a lifetime;
Weeping may last for the night,
But a shout of joy comes in the morning."
—Psalm 30:5

"Weeping Lasts for a Night, Joy Comes in the Morning!"

What brought you to RMI? Please use this space to briefly let our readers know what your life was like when you first found us, Raquel, so our readers understand just what a miracle your restoration is.

Raquel, how did your restoration actually begin?

It all started in September five years ago when during a fight I asked for a separation. It turned out that we did not separate at that time, but I planted a terrible seed. Dear ones, we need to pay a lot of attention to the empty, foolish words we utter because we will have to deal with them in the future. In fact, I asked for a divorce so he would learn a lesson and be afraid of losing me. How silly and stupid. Like so many women, I thought I was being an intelligent, independent woman. But I was following a lie, in fact I was a silly, proud, contentious woman and had been encouraged to be one by everyone. The first person I hurt was my dear HH. I was the exact opposite of the wise woman. I was quarrelsome, proud, destroying everyone around me with my sarcasm brought on by my envy. Time passed after my stupid suggestions, and even though I lived with him, I became more and more contentious and ended up making him and our daughters suffer. So, five years ago, in September, we had another fight and the tables turned—he asked me to leave the house. Suddenly when I realized what I had done, it was too late and I had destroyed my marriage and my entire life.

How did God change your situation Raquel as you sought Him wholeheartedly?

I cried a lot and looked for support in people. Again, I did everything wrong. People had nothing to offer. Only He has Words of Life. All the people I sought for advice told me that there was no way a restoration was possible and that I should give up and move on. They told me that even God does not interfere with a person's free will when it is decided. My husband chose to be rid of me and that was it. Even my family was telling me to go find a new husband and start another family. I was living with my mother and father at that time and I was in my room crying all day. On one of these days, I asked God to help me. If there was a way, a solution to this mess, I asked that He would show me. The first thing that happened was that He started to change my heart so I could hear what He had to say to me. He was calming my heart as I read the Word and He began to keep me company in my room, talking to me and healing my heart. A few days later, I no longer cried. In fact, I smiled again.

What principles, from God's Word (or through our resources), Raquel, did the Lord teach you during this trial?

Once He knew I was ready, the Lord led me to read Erin's book "How God Can and Will Restore Your Marriage" and that was the catalyst that changed me forever. Before, when I read the Bible I did not always understand or know how to apply that Word in my life. Erin's book helped me to better understand all that the Bible says about being a woman who pleases God's heart.

The change began to really happen when I decided to apply in my life all that I found in the Word of God. If I read it in the Bible, I would do it. If I did not read it in the Bible, I would not do it. His Word began to wash away all the anger and pride I had in my heart. Wash me clean and make me new! And suddenly, I became calmer, more delicate, and more humble. I treated everyone with kindness, and all that horrid sarcasm was gone from my heart and lips. How good it was to walk lovingly with the people around me!!!! It seemed like a dream, I seemed like another person, this was not me!!!! It was His love working in my life! My way of being a daughter, a mother, and an employee has changed completely since that day. My greatest joy became simply talking to Him alone in my room, singing love songs to My Beautiful Beloved—He became the great love of my life. Believe it or not, I have changed so much that I don't mind and prefer to get stuck in traffic.

Talking to Him, singing and listening to the Bible on my audio version. It's like listening to God my Father speaking to me.

Another change is that I stopped having lunch with my coworkers. Ungodly talking corrupts good manners. So I began to bring my lunch from home and had lunch alone with Him. I still had time to read and listen to the Bible at lunchtime so I've been able to read through the entire Bible five times already this year. What lovely days I wake up to. I sit in the presence of my HH, warming myself in the Sun of His presence! I learned this in the book "A Wise Woman" along with reading workers@home so I now know how to take better care of my house, and the children. I limit the children's television and increased the hugs, the jokes and the time teaching about what I learned that day, what their Father God wants me to teach them. Such a different life for all of us!

What were the most difficult times that God helped you through Raquel?

The most difficult was to apply the "Let It Go" principle because I hadn't yet had my arms wrapped around my HH. I did not keep calling my land husband or going after him. That was not it. But I'd think about him all the time, dream about him and sometimes found myself shamefully snooping on his facebook and his cell phone.

I knew I had to get him out of my mind and my heart, I had to hand it to Him to finally be able to rest in God. I suffered a lot when I discovered that my earthly husband was talking very badly about me to his family and his friends. Everyone was very supportive of him getting rid of me and offering to help pay for a divorce. He was already dating just weeks after he kicked me out and he had the support of everyone around him to move on and find a decent wife and mother for our children.

I was sick hearing this, but I gave it all into God's hands and I did not confront him (or his family) even during times when they'd be in my face about it. In fact, before my transformation I would have stood up to them, spit in their faces and walked away feeling great satisfaction that I was a strong woman. But today, I have His true love that throws away all the fear and bitterness and I shower myself in His love. His love and His Word washes me of all evil, and leaves me lotioned with His comfort.

At the end of February, two and a half years into my Restoration Journey, my land husband talked to me and asked me to make the divorce official. I heard and remembered everything I learned from Erin about the Word of

God. At the time of that conversation, I was initially sad, more at what it would do to our children. But just as the Word says, weeping will last for a night, but joy comes in the morning!

Raquel, what was the "turning point" of your restoration?

The greatest turning point came when I thought, "I have my HH, so I have everything I need." I woke up the day after my EH asked me to finalize the divorce, (we slept in the same house that night because one of the girls was horribly sick, but we were in separate rooms). Wow, instead of crying, I was happy to have my HH in my life. I started the day by singing a love song of gratitude and then went into look after the girls and care for my mother with all the love He'd showered on me that morning. I prepared a special breakfast and invited My Beautiful Husband to be with us that morning! Meanwhile, my earthly husband seemed to harden his heart more and more. But I was more than all right, I knew He was working. I simply felt a lot of peace in what was to be the final storm.

Tell us HOW it happened Raquel? Did your husband just walk in the front door? Raquel, did you suspect or could you tell you were close to being restored?

My earthly husband was watching my behavior and ten days later came to talk to me and asked me "Are you dating anyone?" I said no, that I was just in a state of peace since my life was in the hands of God. But he kept insisting, he continued to think that I was dating someone because I was very quiet and he said that I was visibly in love with whoever it was. But I really am in love with my HH! That's what he did! But he continued to worry and then two days later, he called me to talk again and said, "I never stopped loving you, and I want you to know I'm very sorry for what I did to you. He said everything is over with the OW and he had made plans for the whole family to be together.

Next, I heard that he changed his Facebook page as married.

We are now living a life I never dreamed was possible. Our home has never been so quiet and peaceful. I know in my heart that I cannot go back to being the person I used to be. My marriage has been restored, yes. Alleluia glory to God!!!!

A few days after my restoration I found myself slipping, starting to say how I was feeling rather than talking to Him about it. So I began fasting again. I fast two days a week to weaken my flesh and strengthen my spirit and I find my love for Him has fully returned.

I still choose to apply the principles of "letting go" and find he has continued to pursue me. Another important thing is that I do not talk too much (knowing that my EH will be won without words) and if I do say anything, I choose words of sweetness (the soft word that's healing to the bones). Above all, I choose to abandon all bitterness, anger and shouting and choose to walk in love. This can only happen when we are filled with His love!

Would you recommend any of our resource in particular that helped you Raquel?

The book *How God Can and Will Restore Your Marriage* and the book *A Wise Woman* were very important to help open my eyes and make me a totally new woman. *Finding the Abundant Life* Course helped me discover my HH. Also what cleansed me from all bitterness and anger was reading through the reading through the Bible and having the Alexandar Scourby app. His Word cleansed me.

Would you be interested in helping encourage other women Raquel?

Yes

Either way Raquel, what kind of encouragement would you like to leave women with, in conclusion?

Dear brides, let your earthly husband go. Do not snoop into his life, do not try to find out what he is doing. Occupy your thought and your life with Him and cleanse your heart by reading through the Bible and discover His love letters to you. He is the only Man capable of making you truly happy. Not only does this allow your flesh to be killed each day, because more of you must leave to give more space for you to receive more of the character of Love of Him in you. Stay in peace, do not give up, keep moving along your journey and in everything, be thankful to the Lord. The closer you are to your HH, the closer you will be to your restoration.

Chapter 13

Constanza

"My God is my rock, in whom I take refuge."
—2 Samuel 22:3

"God is Much More Than Our Pain"

Constanza, how did your restoration actually begin?

It all started when my husband seemed to begin to change from one moment to another. It was like he was an (absent) stranger in our home. Finally, it made sense when I discovered that he was having an affair (the world's term for adultery) and my world fell. So that's when I started looking for help by searching the Internet. Then I found hope when I read *How God Can and Will Restore Your Marriage*.

How did God change your situation Constanza as you sought Him wholeheartedly?

The moment I found your site and I started reading everything. Over and over and over again I read and cried and read more. When I started to do everything the book said, I started praying and fasting so that every day I strengthened myself in God. I was getting closer to the Lord every day too, a relationship that I had neglected but in a way, I never had. Before this journey, He seemed far away and distant, not close to me as I began to know Him.

The closer I got to my HH, the more God did His work. My husband got involved with the OW at work, so each time he left, while fasting, I asked God to get him out of there. To the honor and glory of my God, he was fired. Soon afterward he left his lover when she broke up with him.

After this, he came to me and asked for forgiveness, and of course, I forgave him. Yet now I am praying for a complete healing for my husband and for him to know the Lord as I do. I believe in a God who can do everything, the

God of the impossible. I will not give up on my husband, nor on my marriage because He who began the good work will complete it.

What principles, from God's Word (or through our resources), Constanza, did the Lord teach you during this trial?

Every day, I received encouragement from praise reports and that's what helped me remain happy and God strengthened me. I used the principle of Forgiveness, and that God hates divorce. And that for God there is nothing impossible!!

What were the most difficult times that God helped you through Constanza?

Beloved, there have been so many days of pain, days filled with so many tears. I always read Psalm 23. I read Psalms and Proverbs every day, which is what helped guide me. He also led me to read over all the encouraging marriage testimonies to study what each of these women faced and how they got through their difficulties.

Constanza, what was the "turning point" of your restoration?

It was on the day he asked me for forgiveness, but I had already forgiven him my heart long before he asked. Every day I am surprised by God's attention to details I asked for during my journey that have happened! There are just so many blessings that I cannot explain everything all at once. I regret now at not being careful to submit more journals and sending in a praise every day. If there was one thing I regret, that is it.

Tell us HOW it happened Constanza? Did your husband just walk in the front door?

My husband did not actually leave home. Even though he was still living at home, he would come home very late and left very early so he would not have to see or talk to me. Today he is always very present in our home and already we are planning to begin to travel together, something we haven't done much as a couple since we don't have children yet.

And another thing is God is molding my husband every day. One week before he started doing the Couple's Course, he stayed a week away from home due to his new job so we were not able to start it. Not wanting to nag him, I left it in God's hands. Then one day he said, aren't we going to do the course tonight before going out? I said what course and he said the one that changed you to be so lovely. From that day on it has been one blessing after another. Every day is a miracle!!!

Would you recommend any of our resource in particular that helped you Constanza?

Yes, and I want to be a partner to continue to give towards helping desperate women !!! All the women in the world have to know how to face this misery and to uncover the mystery behind how to save their marriages and help their friends. I recommend and send the first RYM chapter in my emails. So far I have heard back from two friends in crisis and bought them the paperback books. I've already bought a case of your book just to have in my hands to give out, and I'm loving it!!! Thank God for Erin's life. I pray for her and for the mystery behind why so few women know the truth. Please know, you can count on me to help other women. Thank you for everything!!!!

Would you be interested in helping encourage other women Constanza?

Yes, a lot.

Either way Constanza, what kind of encouragement would you like to leave women with, in conclusion?

Girlfriends, do not give up on your husband and your marriage. Because we know that satan's greatest target is the family. We must not forget that the Family is also God's greatest project, which is ongoing. So if we follow our God, learn His principles, find our HH, then God promises to actually change the universe for us in order to Bless us!

What I also want to say is that we're still in the process of restoration because He is never done with either of us. If you just stop learning and changing when your husband comes back to you, then you will miss so many miracles!!! You need to keep moving forward so you don't slip back.

Look, how many of you, imagined your life differently? Think? How much humiliation, shame disrespect did you experience before you wanted to learn about Him and what God says about marriage? Don't let this happen again. Trust in the God who parted the Red Sea. God has a purpose for every trial and a way through the desert, but He would rather we stay in His Promise Land as long as we are fellowshipping with Him and learning His ways.

No matter where you are along your journey, please never think that your situation is more difficult than what God is willing to do for you!!! And stop despairing because there will always be someone, some woman, somewhere in the world who is suffering more than you are. God is much more than our pain, He sent our salvation.

Chapter 14

Jenny

"Everlasting joy will be yours."
—Isaiah 61:7

"Sent Straight From God"

Jenny, how did your restoration actually begin?

My husband left home unexpectedly, breaking my heart by telling me it was over. I was desperately searching the Internet for books or anything to help me understand what was happening and to give me hope that God would bring my husband home. I found Restore Ministries and read your resources for three months, being encouraged before I ordered my own material so I could have books in my hand to pour over.

I received Restore's materials on our anniversary and it turned out that my husband came over that day. He was dropped off and asked me if I wanted to get something to eat. I had read the first chapter of How God Can and Will Restore Your Marriage and it helped me through the dinner. That was the first bit of hope I had since he left April 1, ten months of not seeing or hearing from him! God worked from then on, changing me even more and helping me to be kind and truly forgive. It was a miracle in my heart even though no one could see it.

What principles, from God's Word (or through our resources), Jenny, did the Lord teach you during this trial?

I learned about biblical submission and about trusting God no matter what the situation looks like. I learned to be thankful for very small things, knowing God is faithful to provide what we need when we need it. I learned that ALL things do work together for good for those who love God and are called according to His purpose.

I learned that God won't give me more than I can bear and yet it may be more than I thought I could take. I think I learned to love God above all else. I pray God will continue to give me as many trials as I need to keep me humble and depending on Him—I mean that. Doing it our own way is not peaceful or joyful and He knows it!

How did God change your situation Jenny as you sought Him wholeheartedly?

Doing everything differently. We are taught and told to do things entirely different than His Word says and what we feel like doing, what comes naturally. This is a spiritual journey, not just towards restoration but towards much more. Finding our HH and becoming His bride. No other ministry or church speaks about this and it's why so many woman, like me, clung to and smothers their EH. Making demands rather than finding the Love that we're really looking for.

He helped me repent of my selfishness in our marriage and in general as a selfish person. He helped me to see myself as I was and was there with His mercy for my broken heartedness. I became alive in my trusting Him as never before, even though I had always been excited that He had saved me—not knowing there was so much more I was missing. Being His bride.

It was entirely different to have Him sustaining me like that, as His bride. I was learning so much because His love surrounded me. Interesting too, I did not diet or exercise, but lost a lot of weight and felt better than I had in a long time. This was just an added blessing from my HH. I fasted for the first time and discovered a deeper kind of praying than I had known, actually talking and listening just like having a conversation with Him sitting right next to me.

What were the most difficult times that God helped you through Jenny?

OW and hearing how happy they were. Not hearing from my EH for months and not trying to, which at first was hard. It all changed though when I found my true love. My HH became all I needed or wanted, and as soon as I really lived this way, with no hint of obsession or focusing on my EH, that's when he showed up at my door.

One day after I began hearing from him again we went to lunch and he wound up asking me for a divorce! I did not know how to respond. I ignored my shock but found myself gently disagreeing for a full half hour but then

God brought to my mind to agree with him! So I did. And the moment I did, divorce NEVER came up again! What a test! My husband continued to run from God for another month or so, but then God, in His perfect timing, saved my husband.

After he was saved he came home—we had been apart exactly one year! What a year!

Jenny, what was the "turning point" of your restoration?

It had to have been my focus changing from my EH and not only God the Father, but His Son, who I realized was my HH. Once He became all I needed and wanted, my heart was healed and whole again. With gaping and bleeding hearts, we are not attractive to our husbands, because we are needy and demanding. Once this took place He knew I was ready to be restored. This is what I tell all the women I encourage. Women who run to me instead of to Him can't be restored because if their husband came back, they would begin focusing on and driving him away again.

Would you recommend any of our resource in particular that helped you Jenny?

The resources that I would recommend would include:

How God Can and Will Restore Your Marriage—helped me so much to learn to control my mouth!

The Wise Woman workbook—so much help and hope!

The "Be Encouraged!" tapes—SENT STRAIGHT FROM GOD AND JUST WHAT I NEEDED!!! I did wait to listen until doing the entire workbook, too. I think God blessed me for my obedience.

The workbook and Be Encouraged were the most helpful resources I found.

Tell us HOW it happened Jenny? Did your husband just walk in the front door?

Praise the Lord, my Love has done it! He did the impossible; what everyone said would never happen. I was married for seven years when my husband left. I found out he was involved with another woman, drinking excessively, and they were heavily using drugs. We had attended church together the last few years and he had professed to being saved, which he now says was just an emotional experience.

We do not have children and then the OW became pregnant. However, she had a miscarriage just before my husband left her to come back to me. He said being unfaithful and with another woman was more than he could handle. He planned to leave me and build a family with her prior to this. God used the entire situation to *completely* break me. I lost all interest in everything, but clung to HIM who held me closely.

He gave me a Love song I sang continuously and with His love came the hope I needed when my life was so dark and painful; so much pain that I could not see. Yet my Love showed me compassion and bestowed mercy on my husband too by helping me love him when he was entirely unlovable. Every change was not me doing it. I can't even believe how His love changed me! I began giving love to others rather than needing love from others.

Jenny, did you suspect or could you tell you were close to being restored?

No. I had been so selfish and was not the wife that God wanted me to be, but I didn't know that until I read your resources and He began to gently reveal who I was. I had been through disappointment before, many times, but nothing had ever gotten to me like this painful trial. It was God's timing for me to be His Son's bride. He knew I needed to experience His love, after being broken, in order to change more into the likeness of my first Love.

As I said, my husband did not contact me for the first nine months, because I know that God needed to change me and His faithfulness is what help me not give up. He used Restore Ministries to encourage me. Thank you all. I could not have made it without you. I read and read and read and listened to video after video. I was so dependent on Him and His truths, and although I had a lot of grief when I started, I knew He was sustaining me and that was incredible. He brought me from the bottom and lifted me to the mountain tops!

Then, when my HH became all I wanted and needed, God started to give me opportunities to spend time with my husband after so many months apart. Then, extreme testing followed because he told everyone he would never get back with me because we were miserable together. He kept telling me how far apart we had grown and that I could not see it.

However, I just agreed, although it hurt, then I'd take it to my HH and He'd remind me He was all I needed. My husband also shared things I did not want to know about the OW and that's when I began praying for her, but at first, it was killing me to hear the hold she had on him. But I knew that as I was, I was no better than she was and apart from Him, I would have nothing to offer anyone. God knows this is true.

So, it happened around Christmas, when my husband called crying and I could tell he was in a terrible state. He couldn't understand how I could ever forgive him or how he could have done this to me. He came over that night and slept, but then left the next morning, which surprisingly I was all right with and even was happy about because I had time with my HH. Then he called New Year's Eve (he was alone—PTL!), and we made plans to meet the next day when he asked if he could come home.

Since his returned, we have worked on our marriage, but I struggle now more than when he was gone. I see that clearly it's because of the lack of time and focus I can give to my HH. Yet, I am so thankful for all of it. And I give God glory every chance I can, to share what happened to me with every woman I meet. I explain I overcame huge obstacles and will continue to overcome them, most of which are me and what we women are told to say and act.

Since coming here and I am still learning to this day how to respect my husband (thereby obeying God and His Word), which I had never done before because no one ever taught me or corrected me before this trial. Now when I see that behavior in other women I try to correct them gently and lovingly, which always gives me an opportunity to share Hope At Last and your resources with them. Boasting about my weaknesses is what helps so many women find their way to Him and His love!

I hurt my husband so much, which I never realized until he returned home. As women it's all about us. I know now that he is ordained by God to be given my respect—no question. I want to grow in that way too now that I have my Love by my side. My husband does not drink anymore, and he takes us to church. He even says he wants me to be happy and he tries to encourage me to be closer to the Lord. He'd stopped seeing the OW long before he came home (it was God's mercy on me). So, yes, husbands will also change if we give them room while we focus on our relationship with Him.

My husband is growing and I cannot believe what has happened after our first trials right after he came home. God is so good. My HH is so wonderful. Let me say I am not sorry any of this happened and I expect God to get every drop of glory. Praise God for things just as they are, trusting our Father to do the work as we humbly obey!

Do you have favorite Bible verses Jenny that you would like to pass on to women reading your Testimonies? Promises that He gave you?

"I have told you these things, so that in Me you may have peace. In this world you will have trouble. But take heart! I have overcome the world" John 16:33

"I will go before you, and make the crooked places straight: I will break in pieces the gates of bronze, and cut asunder the bars of iron: And I will give you the treasures of darkness, and hidden riches of secret places, that you may know that I, the LORD, who call you by your name, am the God of Israel." Isaiah 45:2

"Teach us to number our days, that we may gain a heart of wisdom. Psalm 90:12

"But Mary treasured all these things, pondering them in her heart." Luke 2:19

"For truly I say to you, until heaven and earth pass away, not the smallest letter or stroke shall pass from the Law until all is accomplished." Matthew 5:18

Would you be interested in helping encourage other women Jenny?

Yes. I try to help at least one new woman every day. I ask Him to show me who she is and that's when I am able to share your website.

Either way Jenny, what kind of encouragement would you like to leave women with, in conclusion?

No matter what has been thrown at you, it's intended to break you so you'll find your HH and become His bride, washed, healed and whole.

Whether it's drugs, alcohol, an OW or ever if the OW is pregnant, it's all for the purpose of finding Him. And if you're not yet restored it's only because He needs more time to get you ready, but once you are, it will happen quickly so that's why you mustn't waste a single minute. Spend all your time reading and listening to the resources here because it's what He's telling you. Learn to follow His lead, hear His voice above every other. And once you're restored, or better still before you're restored, ask Him to show you other women to help. Then boast about your weaknesses and teach her how to depend on and find Him for herself. Then go find another.

This is a lifelong journey and if you must pray God will continue to give you as many trials as I needed to have to keep me humble and depending on Him—I mean that as I said before.

~ Jenny in Connecticut

Chapter 15

Julie

"For I know the plans that I have for you,'
declares the Lord, 'plans for welfare
and not for calamity to give you
a future and a hope."
—Jeremiah 29: 11-14

"Our Daughter's Illness Made Me Run Back"

What brought you to RMI? Please use this space to briefly let our readers know what your life was like when you first found us, Julie, so our readers understand just what a miracle your restoration is.

Julie, how did your restoration actually begin?

Everything began just two years into our marriage when our daughter was only one. I was still very immature and inexperienced, so when I discovered a betrayal of my husband with another woman, I began to destroy everything. I discovered everything like so many others through a message on his cell phone. I screamed and told everyone that I could that I had been betrayed. I even sent him away, sent him packing, but that same week he came back. He said he'd change, but the problem was I did not change. I decided I was a victim and I always accused him of destroying our marriage.

In fact, at that time, I had not the slightest knowledge that it was I who was wrong. I have always been contentious and argumentative, shouting at him and treating him like a child. I was never once submissive and never respected him as a wife should respect her husband. When he returned, I vowed to make him pay for what he'd done to me. That began my trajectory path of pain and suffering.

Not to anyone's surprise, my husband continued to betray me. By this time our daughter was already three years old and we discovered she had liver cancer (but her healing is another testimony I owe God to write). But I mention this because, since our first betrayal we were both far from the Lord. Even though we met in the church, were both Christians and had made it our lives to serve God as a family. It was our daughter's illness that made me run back to my Savior. In great pain, I realized I was alone and at one point, my EH also came running back to Him. But neither of us surrendered to the Father with all our hearts, so because we continued to make the same errors even this catastrophic event didn't change either of us.

How did God change your situation Julie as you sought Him wholeheartedly?

My EH got involved with another OW which lasted only a few months. I foolishly caused myself more grief because I was always snooping on his cell phone, in his email, and searching his personal photos. So I discovered everything. Once again I got desperate, and this time I called some brothers from our church and asked for "help"—as if some human being in this world could help me in that moment. The pain that I was living was excruciating. This stupid act only made me demoralize my husband more and more before the people we knew and the church we went to. It was then that we changed churches and went to another of the same denomination. We also moved to a different neighborhood where no one knew the history of our failed marriage.

What principles, from God's Word (or through our resources), Julie, did the Lord teach you during this trial?

Even after that, I did not change and I consider this the worst part of my testimony. In this new church I got involved in various ministries, including the Praise Ministry. I really loved being in the house of God. My husband also got involved in church ministry, but again, soon drifted away from God. Foolishly, I kept going to church without my husband because I thought that was the way to get closer to God. Instead, I finished tearing down my own house. I became involved with a man in the Praise Ministry. So the struggles that continued in my marriage became ten times worse than before.

What were the most difficult times that God helped you through Julie?

It was then when I was surrounded by hurt, and hatred myself due to the OM I had in my life. Then I heard that the OW had given birth to a daughter who was my husband's child.

With a log in my own eye, a mile high, I made the worst decision of my life: to take revenge. You see, I was in church and involved in ministries but without the spiritual cover of my husband as my spiritual leader. Yes, I learned this danger in RMI but I ignored it, thinking it couldn't affect me.

Finally, I was able to see my own adultery, against God and against my husband. Immediately, that same week, the preaching in my church was about going to the one you wronged. So I drove to the house of the OW and I confessed everything to him, which made things worse because I believe part of me wanted to hurt him.

He said he would not leave me, but he said that he did not forgive me either—just as I had never forgiven him. After this, though he remained at home, he got a job very far from home and there he got involved with another OW. And again, I made the same mistakes as a contentious, argumentative woman, I logged into his private Facebook, checked his emails, his photos. I discovered everything and again as a deadly cycle, everything was repeated in my life. The crises, the quarrels, and what led to a point of aggression on my part. The real hell I lived was about to get worse.

Julie, what was the "turning point" of your restoration?

So I started to search for help on the internet and my life changed when I discovered the book "How God Can and Will Restore Your Marriage" and a "Wise Woman." I read everything that was there and began to apply it in my life. The teachings in Erin's book were hidden in my heart. I got pregnant with my second child, a boy, It was in a turbulent pregnancy. Even though my husband was farther away from us and I was suffering, suffering, suffering, I kept trying to change the situation in my own strength. Nothing changed, not until I left the church. It was for selfish reasons, I was tired of going alone, and I'd stopped my relationship with the OM and he and his wife moved away.

Soon my husband left this job and this OW, he said he would be faithful to me again if I believed I could do the same. I told him that the OM and I were over and that's when I finally put into practice the teachings of the book. I stopped following, and snooping on my husband and I set him free. I let him go completely, embraced my HH. That's when I was finally free.

Tell us HOW it happened Julie? Did your husband just walk in the front door? Julie, did you suspect or could you tell you were close to being restored?

One day the unexpected just happened. My husband left home to go to work but came back after 10 minutes asking me how much I loved him. He confessed that he had become involved with another OW, but this time it was with a married OW. This time I had not discovered anything, so I was shocked, how could I let it go?

I couldn't but He could. I simply gave it all to Him. The log was finally out of my own eye, I no longer thought myself so clever and always above reproach. Just as His word says, it was my humility that changed the spiritual climate.

The second unexpected event happened when my husband wanted to go to a new church. On the day we visited he asked to speak to the pastor, and then with tears, holding my hand, he confessed his sin of sexual weakness. He asked for God to help him as he slid from the chair and got down on his knees. Then the pastor prayed for us both because I too explained I had succumbed to the same weakness. We are now members of this church. Even though I go under the protection of my spiritual leader, my spiritual meals come from RMI and my closeness to my HH is found in my quiet time with Him.

He has told me on several occasions just how sorry he is for everything he did and that he wants to start a new life. He explained everything I did that displeased him and what he said practically pushed him to get OW. I'm thankful that what he said was exactly everything I've confessed here, the screaming, the way I would treat him like one of my children. Anyway, it all comes down to the contentious and argumentative woman that I've been through all those years and explained that the only way I was able to change was by finding my HH.

Would you recommend any of our resource in particular that helped you Julie?

Though I bought and read all the resources, it wasn't until I went back to RMI and began reading in the daily encouragements about the courses. I changed for the first time during Course 1, understood more in Course 2, was prepared for restoration in Course 3. But when everything changed, when the impossible happened, was during the second week of the *Finding the Abundant Life* Course. I'd even heard how this was "dangerous" for restoration but I read too many restored marriages that said otherwise.

Dear friend, God restored my marriage not because I deserved it, but because He is merciful and infinitely good to me. Your problem may be great, dear sister, but GOD is GREATER than anything— any sin. He will calm the storms in your life if you will only make Him #1.

Would you be interested in helping encourage other women Julie?

Yes, I really want to help other women.

Either way Julie, what kind of encouragement would you like to leave women with, in conclusion?

I still do not feel prepared for the restoration, I continue struggling to let go, shut up, have a quiet and gentle spirit and kindness in my language. This is because I practiced doing things in the flesh for so long. I know I must remain in the RMI courses that help with being intimate with my HH. I am asking God every day to have a closer intimacy with my HH.

More than restoration with my EH, I want to know the voice of my HH, I want to hear Him speak to me. I want to have a relationship with Him above all else. I long to be His bride and I want Him to be my Heavenly Husband because this is where I've found real peace and love.

The process of marriage restoration is not over when your husband comes home, even after he repents. Once he's home is only the beginning. If you don't have Him as your HH, and He truly is, then you and I can't expect to stop our foolishness and spiritual arrogance. We need to continue clinging to the only One who can help us with our lack of forgiveness, our contentiousness. Only He can help us put into practice the wisdom found in the books, lessons and testimonies we have each found here at RMI. Without ongoing support, I would surely continue to push my earthly husband into the arms of yet another OW.

I apologize for the delay in writing my testimony, that is not how I imagined it, but I have too much to thank God for. He is absolutely in love with me, so for His infinite kindness and mercy, because His plans are far better than mine, I needed to make sure I fully confessed everything to all of you.

HERE are my FAVORITE PROMISES OF GOD:

"For I know the thoughts which I have toward you, saith the LORD, thoughts of peace, and not of evil, to give you an end, which ye hope for: then ye shall call upon me, and pray to me, and I will hear them. I will seek you, and find me when you search for me with all your heart. I will be fond of you, says the Lord, and I will change your lot." Jeremiah 29: 11-14

"God is not a man, that he may lie; nor son of man, that he should repent. If he hath promised, will he not do it? or, having spoken, will he not do it." Numbers 23.19

"In this battle you will not have to fight; Stand ye, stand still, and see the salvation of Jehovah to you, O Judah and Jerusalem. Fear not, neither be you dismayed; tomorrow go out to meet them, for the Lord will be with you." 2 Chronicles 20:17

"And he said, Hear all Judah, and ye inhabitants of Jerusalem, and thou king Jehoshaphat, so the Lord says to you, "Do not be afraid, nor be dismayed at this great multitude; powder The battle is not yours, but God." 2 Chronicles 20:15

Chapter 16

Salomé

"It was good for me to be afflicted,
so that I may learn Your decrees."
—Psalm 119:71

"Not Able to Love"

Salomé, how did your restoration actually begin?

I want to begin my testimony by giving all honor and glory to my God Almighty ... because without Him, there is no restoration!!!!!!

I am convinced that my restoration began the moment I let go of my husband completely and focused on God. Since the beginning of my separation I never stopped praying or fasting, but this did not improve my situation, instead things went from bad to worse. What changed everything was after hearing the *How God Can and Will Restore Your Marriage* (RYM) book, about 50 times, someone told me about it. So, I came to the conclusion that I was missing the most important thing!!!!! And that was to put God ahead of everything... no longer putting my restoration as a priority in my life and have complete contentment with my situation.

So, I began to focus more on my relationship with the Lord as my husband, feeling He was right there!!!!!! When things became like a miracle ... it happened all within about 2 weeks when my mother told me that my husband wanted a divorce, but our Mighty God, the heart of my husband can be turned, because God keeps His promises ...

How did God change your situation as you sought Him wholeheartedly Salomé?

Just at the time that I gave my life to God, and then I found my Heavenly Husband (HH), that's when He gave me back my husband, on a Saturday afternoon, coming back through the door as the book says. And not just back but he had changed! We have a much better relationship than before, and every time I begin to fear or doubt about my husband, I begin to pray and talk to the Lord until peace happens and everything is in focus, He is first again.

What principles, from God's Word (or through our resources), Salomé, did the Lord teach you during this trial?

Coming here I learned to feed my soul with as much of Psalms that I could, they are precious. There is no better balm for the soul that to read Proverbs, and there is no better counselor than God alone. There is no better friend than Jesus, for my life depends on being at peace with my dear God through Him as my HH. Also, to begin the day praising HIM. Honestly there is no better life, than the life demanded by God that we are supposed to live. Only this will stop us from being a contentious woman. Only knowing this will show us how to leave our burdens in God's hands and trust Him.

I think my restoration was far greater with my Heavenly Husband than it ever could be with an earthly husband. I certainly never thought to have a better relationship with God, and I never dreamed to have it this way, to have such love for my HH. I'm more in love with Him as my HH that I am with my EH. There is no fuller life without Him. I am not able to love, I learned to love God as He deserves and commands us, to love my HH!!!! And to LOVE HIM above all things and everyone!!!!!!

Salomé, what were the most difficult times that God helped you through?

Yes, I learned that if you want restoration you have to forgive, beginning with my EH but also to forgive all my enemies, including the OW.

What was the "turning point" of your restoration Salomé?

When he came to ask me about coming back. He said he felt his heart telling him to come hope and that he sincerely regretted everything!! Plus, I had always talked so much about him going to church because before coming here I would never miss, but because I let go, he felt he could take me.

Tell us HOW it happened Salomé? Did your husband just walk in the front door?

One day my mother came in through the front door and told me to give God my divorce, and if I did He soon would overturn it.

The next day I get to my apartment and there is my husband asking me to go on a trip with him, then when we come back, I never imagined that he would ask to restore our marriage. Things changed from a crisis of a divorce looming to restoration, from a single moment to the other just that quickly.

Salomé, did you suspect or could you tell you were close to being restored?

After giving it all to God, I soon began to feel less weight; I felt my burden was lighter and I started to feel content and happy in my situation. Then one morning I opened my Bible and went Psalm 21, and I felt such utter joy when I was reading!! It was something indescribable, my heart jumped with excitement because I knew He had taken me to that verse to tell me what was about to happen!!! And it was only two weeks later that I had my restoration!!!

Would you recommend any of our resource Salomé that helped you?

On this point I can be entirely clear!!!!! The best resources is Erin's book RYM because God created this book through her. God blessed so many women because of the time she went through her restoration that gave us all this book. God can and will restore your marriage was a guide for me and what led me to restoration!! May God bless you Erin, and all your family and descendants for making His sheep be turned back to the Shepherd!! This book is a real help to anyone who has any horrible marriage that needs restoration!!!!!

Do you have favorite Bible verses that you would like to pass on to women reading your Testimonies? Promises that He gave you Salomé?

Isaiah 49:23
"And you will know that I am the Lord; Those who hopefully wait for Me will not be put to shame."

Salomé, would you be interested in helping encourage other women?

Yes

What kind of encouragement would you like to leave women with, in conclusion Salomé?

Dear Friend, do not despair, go through the fires of separation because, like me, it will change your life like it did mine!!!! Be ready to leave everything at the Lord's feet!!! Be patient, is my main advice to everyone!!!! And as the RYM book says, if you try to do everything in your strength you will fail because you need to leave it all to God! The book title says it, *How **GOD** Can and Will Restore Your Marriage*! And if you leave it with Him and focus on Him, He alone will restore you!!!!!!! All glory then, all honor will be His forever!

~ Salomé in New Mexico

Chapter 17

Julieta

"A father to the fatherless…,
…is God in His holy dwelling."
—Psalm 68:5

"Clinging to their Father, Insecure"

Julieta, how did your restoration actually begin?

In September my husband and I argued, and it turned ugly because it was a holiday and both of us were drinking too much. We were in the city with my parents, sisters and brother-in-law and the discussion was so ugly that we decided to leave. By this point I had said many things that hurt my EH, a lot, especially that he would not find someone better than me.

Dear Sisters, I regret having been so contentious, murmuring and quarrelsome. I never asked God to calm me, but only humiliated my husband, saying horrible things and also asking for a divorce every time we discussed anything that made me angry.

When we arrived back home and after we both calmed down, he suddenly stopped talking to me. He continued like this, silent, for days and days. That is when I began to notice that he no longer gave me any affection or attention. He only answered the things I asked, so I really started getting concerned. I also noticed that he began to live with the cell phone in his hands.

That's when I became suspicious and asked him if he had someone else. He was threatening to leave the house and go live with his parents. He answered that there was no other person, but that if he had another woman, it would be easier for him. So, I immediately yelled at him saying that his place was here with his family! Another mistake of mine, I did not let him go and basically challenged him to leave me.

By October I had made my biggest mistake. Because I was suspicious of what he was doing, I started to pry into his emails, and I noticed that he had changed the password. After I finally found a way to break into his email account, I noticed several emails from him to the OW. The emails went back for almost a month where I saw he was communicating with a coworker of his. Sisters, you cannot imagine how I reacted!!! Instead of being quiet and once again seeking my Lord, No, I made the foolish mistake of going out and telling all my friends and relatives that I was being betrayed and cheated on by my husband ... Oh, sisters, every day I pleaded with God, Please forgive me my Lord for being so contentious and for helping to change me!!!

That's the point when I kicked him out of our house, and he left and went to live with his parents. I was in utter despair, but instead of asking for the help of my Master, I went to talk to my cousins, my friends, and the priest of my parish. And they all said the same thing, that I should ask my husband for a divorce, because "God said the only time there could be a divorce would be through fornication." And since I did not understand this verse correctly, because since my God had allowed us to marry, why would He want to separate us ... So, instead of discovering the truth, I started to ask God to put another man in my life so I would forget my husband—can you imagine?

Sisters, thankfully, after I found there was really no other man out there for me, I started searching the internet for what I believed would help. I searched for various prayers sites that would make my husband come home, but nothing I found was any good, because I was not being transformed and from what I shared, you know how God needed to remake me!! And that didn't happen until I was finally broken and He led me here to RMI.

How did God change your situation Julieta as you sought Him wholeheartedly?

In my time of desperation, once I was broken, I went to Google to search for Marriage Restoration and it was then that God led me the RMI website and I began to read the book *How God Can and Will Restore Your Marriage.*

Sisters, it was the greatest gift I received in my life! At that moment of utter anguish and despair, I could finally see the truth. Until that moment I had only seen my EH mistakes, but after reading the chapters, I began to see what I'd done wrong. All the things about myself I'd never seen before and

I was very ashamed to put it mildly. So, I began my journey by asking for forgiveness for my actions, first asking God, then everyone I'd hurt or contacted speaking badly and revealing the sins of my husband—instead of confessing my own!

Then, I began to follow everything that the book taught me, mainly to Read the Word of my Lord, something that I had never done. Also, to always seek God first and to follow His word, which none of my Christian friends or priest had ever said to me.

What principles, from God's Word (or through our resources), Julieta, did the Lord teach you during this trial?

The first principle I started with, as I said, was to ask my God for forgiveness for my actions and also all the people with whom I spoke about my husband. To confess to them saying that I was a contentious, murmurous and horribly quarrelsome woman and that the biggest culprit of all this mess in our marriage was me.

I also began to search God's word about everything in my life, and to Praise Him and Glorify Him at all times with prayers and love songs! This led to me letting go of my Facebook and all other social networks since we are supposed to be women who are gentle and quiet, happily at home where the temptations don't overtake us.

Also important, I let my husband go and made it clear to the point of not just saying it, but where I no longer contacted him. During this time he did not call or send emails or an SMS. After some time, he would send me an email and I answered as gently as possible without saying any more.

When he began to show up at our house or he called me, I always treated him tenderly. Then when he began to come and wanted intimacy, I was quietly submissive. Each time I let my HH and EH take the lead, submitting to my HH and to my EH in that order.

What were the most difficult times that God helped you through Julieta?

We have twin daughters who are 3 years old (I sent you a picture) and it's when I saw how much they were clinging to their father and that they'd become so insecure. Seeing them suffer because of the distance of their daddy, made me very sad. They were never happy, never smiling (not like they are now!).

During this time, due to my prior contentiousness, I had to be their mother and their father. I had them both on my lap, when before they would both sit on his lap. During this time he only called them once in awhile and showed up on a couple of weekends a month to take them to his mother's house. During these times I was alone at home, and at those times is when I often found myself feeling like I was battling a martyrdom mentality. To rid myself of this, I clung to my Lord, reading His word in the Bible and being consoled as I'd crawl in my heavenly Father's lap.

Julieta, what was the "turning point" of your restoration?

The turning point was when I began to follow the steps that the book taught me because I was lost and this amazing book taught me to seek God always and put Him in first place and that I realized that all my questions— He answered me—through the many Biblical passages and also through my daughters (the things they said to me I knew were sent by Him).

One morning, at dawn, I felt a great desire to pray for my earthly husband and the OW and that's when it happened.

Tell us HOW it happened Julieta? Did your husband just walk in the front door? Julieta, did you suspect or could you tell you were close to being restored?

I was feeling this overwhelming need to pray for not just my EH but also for the sake of the OW. It was late the same day when he texted me on my cell phone saying, "Why don't you fight for our marriage? Why are you giving up on us?" Wow, when I read this message, it was with great joy, for I knew my Lord was breaking my husband's heart. And soon after that, he broke up with the OW and started to come to our house. One day he came and ask me to pray for him. We'd been Catholic and soon he started to ask me to go to church with him on Sundays.

Once he came home for good, he still was not wearing our wedding ring and he had not told me "I love you." But my faith was unshakeable, and I believed that my Lord will definitely Restore Our Marriage fully!

It took a few months of keeping my focus on my HH and telling Him He was all I wanted or needed. Then one day he just walked into our bedroom and took my hand, saying I LOVE YOU and then he showed me his hand where I saw the wedding ring I'd once placed on his finger was back there!

Would you recommend any of our resource in particular that helped you Julieta?

Yes, everyone should start with *How God Can and Will Restore Your Marriage* and then go through *A Wise Woman* to get ready for restoration since this is when I found it most difficult. What helped too was to read and mark *By the Word of Their Testimonies*, to help overcome the feelings that my restoration might never happen. My favorite was Finding the Abundant Life Course because it helped me have Someone Love me the way I needed to be loved and so I could love my EH during the difficult times.

In addition, was the Encourager that was my form of fellowship as I got off social networks.

May I say that I will remain here at RMI and tithe here to receive the truth for the rest of my life. And lastly, may I again point to the book *How God Can and Will Restore Your Marriage* because as I said, it was the greatest gift I received in my entire life, helping me through the worst and most difficult time I was going through. Please consider giving this gift to your family and friends.

Would you be interested in helping encourage other women Julieta?

Absolutely!!!!!!

Either way Julieta, what kind of encouragement would you like to leave women with, in conclusion?

Firstly, to seek God and Love your HH above everyone and everything else! Be sure you do everything that His word says and Do not talk to anyone about your situation, speak only to God! Stop asking Him for the Restoration of Your Marriage, but Let GO and let Him do it, asking only for His Will for your life! Ask Him for your transformation!

May God make you into a Virtuous Woman, a Wise Woman, who builds her house on the Rock so that nothing and no one will overthrow you!!

Chapter 18

Olive

"for we are sure that we have a clear conscience,
desiring to act honorably in all things."
—Hebrews 13:18

"Place of Honor"

Though the marriage I am about to share with you wasn't in trouble, it does have significance due to how many women are finding themselves facing what Olive faced with dignity and "smiling at the future." I was blessed to be able to get to know Olive by way of her being an extended family member. My daughter-in-law mentioned one day that her brother's wife, her sister-in-law, was looking for more houses to clean. Though I'd always had many of my own children helping me clean, with so many already married, with just as large a home to clean, I felt the pull to hire her when I sought God about it.

Right away I saw how Olive was so good. She was very quiet and also worked diligently each week she came. Later, after she was done, I found myself just talking to her (with me doing almost all the talking), just like I'd talk to my own daughters. I felt badly for keeping her when I knew she had a little boy she needed to get home to, but when I spoke to the Lord about helping me just to let her leave after she was done, it never failed that we would just talk, sometimes for hours. I didn't know much about Olive or her past, but I had heard how she stayed with her husband when he went through some pretty tough times (though I never heard or asked to hear all the details). So I had always admired her inner strength and because the only topic I'm really passionate about is the Lord, I just assumed she was a Christian.

What I didn't know is that my own DIL, and her own mother, had been praying for Olive. For her to come to know and experience the Lord. It was only later that I understood that God was using me to water the seed they'd planted. It was just by being a friend and loving her (paying her well and tipping her generously also went a long way to maybe her sticking around a while ;) and simply talking about how intimately my HH played a role in every aspect of my life. Eventually, she told me they were moving, and when she told me, we even discussed her driving back every other week, but the Lord was done with watering the seed—He was about to bring about His harvest!

Olive had to face something that would have been impossible without her having a deep relationship with Him. What happened right after they moved, and what continues to this day, still astounds me! Olive's husband, my DIL's brother, was contacted by an old girlfriend on Facebook— who said she'd had his baby! A little boy who was just a little older than Olive's precious little boy who was a toddler. DNA proved he was the father, but that only confirmed what Olive told her husband the moment she'd heard. Not only did Olive want her husband to support his little boy financially (even if it meant that Olive would need to clean more houses), but she wanted to embrace this little boy as a real son to her and her husband. Because he had a mother, the former girlfriend of her husband's, she didn't want this former girlfriend to feel threatened, so she'd invite BOTH of them to their home for every holiday! Olive even bought a Christmas stocking for their mantel (I saw it!) and also noted that this son's stocking was right next to her husband's stocking—even before her own son (since he was older than her son), giving him a place of honor!

Soon after welcoming this little boy and his mother into their family, they welcomed another baby boy to make this three cord of sons even more special. I've seen pictures of Olive since then, and her face glows! This story of restoration is witnessed by so many who know the whole story and are equally amazed by Olive and wonder how she could do it.

There are many women who come to this ministry who are asked to go through something similar (though as we know, no two restoration journeys are ever exactly alike). But there are only few who are willing to accept this path as graciously or as lovingly due to them not understanding the blessings that come with being called to go through trials like this. My hope is that you will share this with many other women, sending them the link in order to help them with what they may be facing or will be asked to deal with in their future.

True, accepting this IS impossible, but not when you look deeply into His face. Only then can you "smile at the future" knowing whatever He sends us, in whatever form, will always have a blessing hidden within the tragedy if we will only take the time to look for it.

Chapter 19

Erika

"Has He said, and will He not do it?
Or has He spoken, and will He not make it good?"
—Numbers 23:19

"Challenging and Wonderful Journey of Your Life!"

What brought you to RMI? Please use this space to briefly let our readers know what your life was like when you first found us, Erika, so our readers understand just what a miracle your restoration is.

Erika, how did your restoration actually begin?

It all started when I realized that my husband was moving away from us emotionally. He began building a life apart from ours as a family. I saw that his friendships were with single guys, and his work environment often ended by going out and partying.

When I saw this happening, I started becoming irritated and depressed, in such a way that I too went to live my own life. I began going out alone or with our children. Making friends with mothers of their friends, spending a lot of time with these friends (and most of the time drinking, gossiping and talking badly about our husbands!). In addition, I alone remained faithful to attending Sunday services, by myself or with our children.

Then someone gave me the book "How God Can and Will Restore Your Marriage". My life changed the moment I read it. Then I read it over and over again!

I was able to start applying the principles immediately, especially "letting go" because I was consumed by looking for my husband. I was so desperate that had it not been for this wise counsel, I would have driven him away for good.

In fact, even without knowing His word at all in the beginning, "getting out of the way of the sinner" made a lot of sense to me! I wanted to obey the God who stretched out His hand to save me and save my family! So, Hallelujah, from that moment I stopped pursuing him and ultimately found Him—my HH!

Reading those words in Erin's book I could recognize myself, recognize my mistakes and understand what was happening and the mess I had made of my life! I saw that I was not alone and that God had a perfect plan for me!

How did God change your situation Erika as you sought Him wholeheartedly?

During the holidays, I tried to plan a family trip - in fact, I was always the one who did everything, and especially to plan this vacation. I knew the crisis in our marriage was very serious, we did not understand each other at all!

Even though we agreed to take the vacation, my husband did not want to go, but I insisted. I fought him on this. I tried blackmail, I tried being the victim of the situation, crying, and saying how he was making me suffer. But he'd had enough—my husband did not care anymore! And so I then told him that I would pay for the trip! So, against his will, we went!

He had already warned me that he would take us, but he would not stay with us and then he would just come back to get us after the vacation. Although I'd gotten my way, the vacation was days with a mixture of joy and fun with my children along with deep sadness. I knew something very bad was going to happen. Something different, something scary was happening and I was right. The culmination of my bad behavior showed up in a message from my husband saying he could not come back to get us!

The pain I felt was huge. I remember walking into the ocean and crying non-stop, begging God to save me and save my family! I looked at the enormity of what had happened and I knew I would have difficult moments ahead and I needed God more than ever by my side!

Today I realize that God began His work there, on that day. Before, I was living a life filled with thoughts of hopelessness. I began to feel that God would act in my situation ... and I was able to begin my journey for my children. For the first time, I began to feel some hope for my marriage.

When I got home, I thought my husband would be expecting us and at least would have missed the children, but that was not the case. He was late and indifferent that day towards all of us.

From then on, things only got worse. I discovered the existence of an OW and without a thought— I threw everything in his face! I felt so lost and confused that I decided to look for a psychologist to help me be different and face what was ahead!

I remember that during my consultation, I began to identify my mistakes and she told me that I could not feel that way and that the culprit was my husband.

After my first consultation, I had the worst argument with my husband! The psychologist told me that I should feel anger and that I should demand that he choose whether it was me or OW he wanted to be with. My husband has not returned home this day ...

God was already showing me how I had been contentious and built my home on the sand and did not climb the Rock! And in his infinite love, He was already showing me that only with Him could I face what was happening.

On a morning of despair as I walked aimlessly, lost and praying, asking God to help me, even though my family gave me "strength" so that I would abandon my husband - because they knew I was suffering! I knew there was something bigger reserved for us!

This morning. I heard, "God of covenant, God of promise, God who is not man to lie ...". I went to church, crying and asking for counsel. Thank God, the priest who talked to me, gave me hope, but I need more! I need to know what to do!

What principles, from God's Word (or through our resources), Erika, did the Lord teach you during this trial?

It was when I began hearing of a testimony about someone's healing that I thought, there must be testimonies of restored marriages! And so I found the RMI site and began to read that it was possible! God be praised!

I studied them each week as they came in on the Encourager and went back looking at similarities of each one. What I saw was that those who found peace right away and then had a restored marriage found and fell in love with their HH, so that is what I told Him I wanted too!

What were the most difficult times that God helped you through Erika?

The most difficult times the Lord helped me to go through were with my children who asked for their father. They're worry for him caused them to become sick all the time. I held on so as not to cry and when I asked my HH what to do, He gave me encouragement in the RMI material. I read that a mother told her children that daddy was solving things that only he could solve and that as soon as possible, he would return home! Thank you, my sister, who shared these wise words, because they comforted my children too!

Besides this difficulty, there were also my parents who suffered with me. I know that they were very worried, yet HE helped me to comfort them and despite everything, I did not complain about anything to them or anyone. I had my HH to go to and that was enough. I also learned not to ask them for anything and of course, God took care of everything. I was never alone, nor will I ever be alone or without help. I will always and forever go to my HH!!

Erika, what was the "turning point" of your restoration?

The turning point in my situation was the moment I started applying the principles of "letting go" and "winning without a word." And, of course, this was possible when I embraced my HH and put both my hands into His. This was the key because my husband said to everyone right away that I was behaving differently! And actually that I was glowing, which made him nervous there was someone else.

One day he sent me a message saying: "You do not call me anymore, what happened?" Brides, this change happened right after one of the lessons on the letting go, when I asked and told my HH that I really wanted to let go and look only to Him! He was all I wanted and needed. A moment later I heard a ding and there was the message on my cell phone! God is wonderful when we become His Son's bride!

Tell us HOW it happened Erika? Did your husband just walk in the front door? Erika, did you suspect or could you tell you were close to being restored?

Yes, in fact, I just realized my marriage has been restored, even though this all happened some time ago! Yes, I was deceived because I always dreamed of telling my restoration as a love story, where my husband came back begging me for forgiveness. It didn't happen that way so I thought it wasn't actually restored!

My husband left home one day, not saying what he was doing, took some clothes he'd hidden, after telling me that we had made a great mistake in getting married! He told me everything was wrong between us, that we did not mesh as a couple should. He said my family would not accept him and many other things. Yet, at this time he was actually involved with another woman!

Soon after I found the book by Erin, and immediately began to apply the principles, everything began to change. Suddenly one day I heard a noise in the door lock and I saw my husband coming into the house! My kids ran screaming "Daddy, Daddy, Daddy." Seeing this brought tears to my eyes because I know He had him come back for my children, not me because I felt fully loved by Him! I still hear my little boy say, "Daddy, you disappeared and I was so homesick for you!" So sweet. My husband sat down and hugged them both and I saw tears streaming down his face! He was sad and confused, and never really said much to me.

At that moment, I did not thank him as I'd planned so many times in my head when I used to dream of my restoration. But I thanked God and my HH.

Had this happened like this, before I met my HH, I am honest when I say my heart would have turned to stone. Before my HH I wanted and demanded so much more from my EH. I would have wanted hugs and beautiful words, but thankfully, and I know you brides would agree with me, that our HH gives us loving words and hugs every moment of every day!

Had I had the "model" restoration that I created for myself before meeting Him, I would have failed to understand what is says in Isaiah 55:8–9: "'For My thoughts are not your thoughts, neither are your ways My ways,' declares the Lord. 'For as the heavens are higher than the earth, so are My ways higher than your ways, and My thoughts than your thoughts.'"

And I love how the Message Bible says it," I don't think the way you think. The way you work isn't the way I work. For as the sky soars high above earth, so the way I work surpasses the way you work, and the way I think is beyond the way you think."

"Just as rain and snow descends from the skies and don't go back until they've watered the earth, Doing their work of making things grow and blossom, producing seed for farmers and food for the hungry, so will the words that come out of my mouth not come back empty-handed. They'll do the work I sent them to do, they'll complete the assignment I gave them."

In the end, my husband was away from home for less than ten months, but the days were long days, and so intense— until I found my Bridegroom. Then the moment I found Him things changed.

He, through this Ministry, gave me the understanding that I started the Journey of my entire life and I do not, will not, go back! After all, where could I go? Nowhere He isn't. His whispers to me the words of eternal life and abundant living!

I continue my Journey with Him at my side, holding my hand. And for those who are still seeking restoration, stop. Seek Him, your HH. Because just as Erin says, the more and more that I approach Him, my HH, the more my husband approaches me and wants me! But at any time I take his eyes off my HH and trust my own understanding or try to please my husband— immediately my husband moves away from me!

Our hearts must be fully His and this is something you can't fool God about. He knows and tests your heart to know if you're ready for restoration. Are you ready?

Would you recommend any of our resource in particular that helped you Erika?

Start with *How God Can and Will Restore Your Marriage* then go to *A Wise Woman* next. Study all the *Testimonies*, and go through online courses. When you're ready to open your heart to your HH it will happen by reading *Finding the Abundant Life* Course.

The book A Wise Woman is so practical and has specific teachings for a woman who wants to be ready for her husband when he returns, to be the wife that pleases God!

I highly recommend the courses as I said and reading the Encourager blog. Oh, how could I have started the day without that encouragement! And besides reading, I highly recommend that you write your praise reports and not wait. Pouring out your hearts into praise to your HH not only helps other women, it makes God take notice of you. Share how He is transforming you through His love! How He cares for you.

Would you be interested in helping encourage other women Erika?

Yes. Thank God today I know there is no greater joy in helping other women! Sending them to HopeAtLast and encouraging them to continue on their journey. To not ask me but ask HIM!!

Either way Erika, what kind of encouragement would you like to leave women with, in conclusion?

God has a perfect plan for your life! And this plan is unique, it's special for you! Yet, for all of us brokenhearted women, His plan begins with finding our HH. He is the Beloved of our souls, is anxious to be kind to you, to pour His love on you and be your HH in every way! Many of you have been chosen and will be blessed with the restoration of your marriage because He has promised and He is faithful! Believe! Get busy being ready for the most challenging and wonderful journey of your life: your Restoration with HIM!

Chapter 20

Joanie & Doug

"A broken and a contrite heart,
O God, You will not despise."
—Psalm 51:17

"Just Remarried"

Six months ago, I called the publisher of the RYM that I found in the front of the book, Mt. Zion. I'd called to let them know that they sent me the *How God Can and Will Restore Your Marriage* by Erin Thiele about a year prior and I wanted them to know how this book affected my life. My husband and I had been divorced for nine years and in all those years, I had not seen or heard from him. I didn't know where he was living, if he'd remarried or even if he was still alive. I explained that I'd just felt like I should ask for this book along with a few other books Mt. Zion offered for free, and then when I got it I just felt like reading it for some reason. And just as I do with all the books I read from, I decided to believe what it said because of so much of the book being simply God's word, His promises. I decided that if those promises were for everyone, then maybe those promises were for me too.

The promises stuck with me and I was also wondering how I'd stumbled on to this book when I wasn't unhappy with my life at all, and I never considered reuniting with my husband after we mutually separated. Then one day something amazing happened, I got phone call and it was from my ex-husband. And this is exactly what he said, "I called to tell you that I am interested in restoring our marriage." Then he asked me, "What do you think?" Quite honestly, I really couldn't think at all, I was simply too stunned to think or say anything. So much for my faith believing He is the God of the impossible.

When my ex and I met, I took my book out of my purse and showed it to my ex and explained about the promises. That's when he opened his bible and showed me that many I highlighted were the very same verses He had marked in his bible!!!

So, I called your publisher (over and over actually) thanking them for their part in helping to get *How God Can and Will Restore Your Marriage* into the hands of those who need hope, even when they don't know they are looking for hope!!

Praise the Lord! We were remarried in Hawaii with our two sons who sang at our wedding. So please pass this on to Mrs. Thiele and let her know I just had to write to thank her personally for what she's done for our family!!

~ Joanie & Doug in Delaware, RESTORED

Chapter 21

Roberto

"For all the promises of God
find their yes in Him."
—2 Corinthians 1:20

"Yes! Yes!! Yes!!!"

First, a Praise Report From Roberto in Brazil:

Thank you for everything you helped me learn in this great course. God is now leading my life and finally, my marriage restoration, in His time.

I would recommend that every man studies your free course—every man going through crises in their marriage. It's not enough to just *read* the book, journaling has changed me and my marriage. I'm not sure why every man doesn't do it since it's free.

Before coming here my life was a mess. I was seeking aid from everyone, then on the Internet, I found this site. I filled out my questionnaire to access the course online since I'd heard such good things about it. I was living a life of despair and deep depression. This course is helping me a lot and I have much more hope now once I began to journal daily.

My Lord thank you for directing me to this site. Thanks for helping me in a difficult time of my life and for changing me. I know Your providence made me find this Ministry. I'm am finally reaping joy by your grace the more I invest into learning the truth.

Note: Roberto donated to pay for his course and another man in need and wants to tell him:

"My brother, you who are going through a dark valley or perhaps living in a time where you do not realize the hope there is still left if your marriage, but just know and trust that there is. Trust in GOD to do it. He is the Lord of all things. He is the God of the impossible. God bless you as you study this course!

Now, Roberto's RESTORED Marriage Testimony:

Roberto, please tell us how the crisis in your marriage started?

I realized there was a crisis one day when I was in the city where my wife was working. This city was 6 hours from our residence and I went after her in May. I thought we were about to resume our relationship, but it was there that she confessed to me that she was involved with another man. Three days after my wife had asked for the separation, I was fired from my job. I lost everything in a week. All this was the beginning of God moving in my life.

Today I realize that the Lord protected me a lot during the revelations that my wife did, about this new relationship and her reasons for separation. It was a very bad day, it seems that the world had fallen on top of me.

Early that same day I said a prayer, "My God, My Lord, forgive me for my mistakes and sins. Please hear me, I do not want another family, I want this family you gave me Lord." And I see that it was right after this prayer that God led along the correct paths to get to my restoration.

It wasn't due to what my wife had done, in being with this other man (OM). No, all this happened because I was very disobedient to God. I say this, because, for 13 years of relationship with my wife (including dating, engagement, and marriage) I committed adultery, gave into the temptation of prostitution, I was rude, I gave room to the devil, to alcoholism and allowed pornography coming into my marriage and other things that displeased God.

That's what attracted me to God, my Father and to a unique experience for those who want to live in God's presence in their lives. I have always been a "religious" man, always been Catholic, but I was a Pharisee. I was a false prophet, although I was a minister of the Word and a preacher of the Word of God I'd still be completely disobedient to God—but praise the Lord, He has drawn me to HIM during this tribulation. Because if it were not so, I would still be in dangerous error to this day.

Next, Roberto, please tell our readers, how did God change you & your situation as you sought Him wholeheartedly?

The Lord put a desire in my heart to seek testimonies of restored marriages and find out if this would be possible. I even saw some testimonies, but it didn't interest me much because I was very troubled and disgusted with the whole situation in my own life. But then God guided me to a couple of friends I have. And while talking to the wife of my college friend I made a decision to fight for my marriage.

His wife was an instrument in God's hands. It was through talking to her that God showed Himself to me and conveyed His word to me.

During this conversation, she said, "GOD WILL NOT DESTROY A FAMILY TO BUILD ANOTHER." And after hearing this word I decided to look for more testimonies of restored marriages and to fight for my own marriage. God led me to find a restoration family website that was very good and ended up leading me to the RMI website. And then a friend, who is also on this walk for his own marriage, sent me the book *How God Can and Will Restore Your Marriage*. This book was the turning point in my life. When I started reading the testimonies, the praise reports, I subscribed and began to take the courses for men in my own language, Portuguese. I ended up doing all of them, all 3 courses you offer men, even though the ones I first found were directed to women.

All this led me to seek God even more as a Father. The "Psalms" and "Proverbs" taught me to PRAY to God. During my search towards God— the Lord has transformed me. It was during this crisis that I had my first real and personal encounter with Jesus Christ.

I confess that I fell many times during this journey, but each of these falls is what He used to make me look more to God for my healing and deliverance.

What are the principles, from God's Word (or through our resources), did the Lord teach you during this trial Roberto?

The main principle was to have the grace to read the Scriptures more often and believe more in them. And also reading the books and taking the courses that RMI offers us, they are full of truths of God's Word that help you grow spiritually like none I've ever found.

All these materials have taught me to live an intimate relationship with God as my Father and to have a personal relationship with the Lord. It's like nothing I've ever experienced before. All this led me to love God above all else, something I didn't do before.

The other principle was practicing the LETTING GO. It is necessary, even though it's difficult. It is this principle that makes you take your hands off things so that God's hand becomes sovereign over all the situations or circumstances in our lives.

That's what I did **and** when I started applying it to my life, I obtained several victories. The secret is LETTING GO of everything to God is critical.

The word of God that caught my attention the most in this journey was:

"Rejoice always, pray continually, give thanks in all circumstances; for this is God's will for you in Christ Jesus. Do not quench the Spirit. Do not treat prophecies with contempt but test them all; hold on to what is good, reject every kind of evil." 1 Thessalonians 5: 16-22

Roberto, what were the most difficult times that the Lord helped you through?

I realize that the most difficult times was at the beginning of the whole situation; when you find out about the other person in your spouse's life. And when you discover, through God's hand, that the error was totally YOURS. But when you start to learn and to understand, according to the word of God, and experience a relationship with God, the Lord protects our hearts from everything.

I say this because God protected me from everything, even when she said she did not love me anymore, and that she had found in another man what she did not find in me.

Please, help our readers to know if you suspected you were close to restoration. Were there any signs Roberto?

I did not suspect anything because things just got worse. Humanly speaking there was no hope.

Roberto were there other "turning points" during your restoration that you didn't already mention?

What I said before I can't say strongly enough. The turning point was when I started practicing the Letting Go principle. I said this always in my prayers, that I did not want to worry about the situation anymore and **just let it go**. I started to pray to God asking Him to deliver me from the DESERT because I couldn't bear that situation anymore.

I wanted to live the best of God because all I was experiencing and learning always led me to GOD'S FAITHFUL LOVE to humanity. And I knew that God's decision would be the best for me. Whether or not He chose to restore my marriage wasn't my main goal. This is about TRULY RELYING ON OUR FAITHFUL GOD. That was the phrase that I stuck to, and still do, GOD IS FAITHFUL and so is His plan for our lives.

If you would, Roberto, carefully explain just HOW it happened: Did your wife contact you by phone or just show up at your home?

I did not suspect anything because since May, when we signed the divorce, things have only become worse. She even asked me to take all my belongings out of the house, but whenever I tried to do that something happened to stop it.

Then, nine months later, in February, things actually got worse. She started showing her new relationship in social networks, according to a friend of mine, and then her father asked me to take my stuff out of the house. Then I felt obliged to do so within 60 days. Our house is on top of the house of my father-in-law.

I know that in that same month God put a desire in my heart to pray more for my wife, which I was not doing any longer; I'd stopped as part of my letting go. And this desire came to me one month before our restoration, which took place the following month.

My wife asked my mother-in-law to call me and say that she (my wife) would like to talk to me and in that same day the LORD DID HIS WORK OF RECONCILIATION AND DECLARED HIS VICTORY IN OUR LIVES. We should always say to HIM," Amen! Praise and glory and wisdom and thanks and honor and power and strength be to our God forever and ever. Amen!" Revelation 7:12

Based on your own restoration, would you recommend any of our resource in particular that helped you, Roberto?

Everyone in a marriage crisis needs to get the book *How God Will Restore Your Marriage* and give it to friends and family in marriage crises. It will not only restore but it will also help them to find the Lord. Next, the *A Wise Man* and *A Wise Woman* for your wives. The courses, really help to keep you moving forward daily and to journal your heart and feelings to the Lord that really begins to change your life in amazing ways. I also would suggest the Encourager.

NOTE: For couples, we have a new couples course for husbands to lead and spiritually feed your wives.

Would you be interested in helping to encourage other men?

YES! YES! YES!

Either way, Roberto, what kind of encouragement you would like to leave for men, in conclusion?

Ladies and gentlemen, first of all, believe in God because nothing is impossible with Him, see Luke 1:37. And everything that this ministry says, and shares is true and powerful by God's grace.

And the word of God is true. Read what it says:

"The man who hates and divorces his wife," says the Lord, the God of Israel, "does violence to the one he should protect," says the Lord Almighty. So be on your guard, and do not be unfaithful." Malachi 2:16) This is true because God did not allow the advancement of my divorce, which was already signed. He restored us before it took place, and we canceled it.

Today my wife talks about what happened to her during that period and I feel amazed because God does not act only in our lives, but He also acts in the life of the rebellious spouse. The change is completed in the Lord's time; **first** to you and then to your loved one.

I say this to you in closing, do not give up. God really hears our prayers, because my separation took one year and ten months. He is always by our side and, even if the circumstances are not agreeable to us, it is because the LORD is acting in our behalf.

Please experience the power of LET GO OF EVERYTHING TO GOD no matter what crisis or difficulty you're going through. It is the only way for God to take over and do the impossible.

Update: Roberto and his wife were blessed with a baby daughter, Giovanna, born 16 months after their restoration—after trusting God for their infertility—after reading A Wise Man Course "The Fruit of the Womb"!!!

Chapter 22

Natasha

"My sheep hear my voice, and
I know them, and they follow me."
—John 10:27

"A Healthy Baby"

What brought you to RMI? Please use this space to briefly let our readers know what your life was like when you first found us, Natasha, so our readers understand just what a miracle your restoration is.

Natasha, how did your restoration actually begin?

My EH left me for the second time whilst I was pregnant with our child. He had left two years before that but returned. I felt finally we could start rebuilding our marriage, but I did not put God first and my marriage was still a very big idol. I worshipped it, sought my identity, success, and future in my husband and marriage. The first time I needed restoration, I was with a stander ministry and pretty much "prayed him home" without making any of those necessary and critical changes that needed to happen to me.

I was a contentious and rebellious wife, know it all and very much a Pharisee. I knew what was best for my husband and did not appreciate his intelligence, character or intentions. I knew that the scriptures stated that we should submit to our husband in everything. Yet, in my heart, I questioned this commandment—my thoughts would go like this," Really in everything?". I never realised that I was to submit to God *through* my husband and that I was not really questioning my husband's authority but I was questioning God's authority (just like in the garden when the devil asked Eve, "Did God actually say that?").

Prior to my separation, I eventually began to submit, but only grudgingly and in rebellion because I now realised that I did not trust God 's order and wisdom. I did not trust that God was sovereign and can arrange things His way. I felt I needed to help God and was deceiving myself that I was a helpmate. Ultimately, I took God totally out of the equation.

Anyway, as soon as I became pregnant, my husband could not stand me, he moved into a separate room and did not want to have anything to do with me. He became very harsh, distant, and constantly blamed me for everything. He stopped communication and started asking me for a separation.

One day we had an argument where things got heated and we both felt we couldn't go on with the marriage. I cannot remember everything I said on that day, but I remember saying I cannot do this anymore and that he could leave if he wanted to leave. I said this after he told me that marrying me was the biggest mistake of his life. Then he moved out.

I was heartbroken, wondering how I was going to care for four children by myself. I was able to let go physically but it was so difficult letting go emotionally and psychologically.

How did God change your situation Natasha as you sought Him wholeheartedly?

Right from the start, I was able to let go physically but emotionally and psychologically, I was unable to let go. Then God started changing my heart. You see, I joined a stander ministry following the first separation over two years before. Whilst I believed at the time that God would restore my marriage, I struggled with the standers ministry because I also believe in letting go and their ministry is based on pursuing the prodigal. The Bible states that "he who finds a wife" so it's the man who should pursue. I believe there is really no point in pursuing a man aggressively. It was in the turmoil of knowing that God wanted to restore my marriage but not knowing the practicalities involved that God led me to this ministry.

As soon as I got to this ministry and read the first page of HopeAtLast.com, I knew that God had directed my steps. I was convicted of my sin, I cried and sobbed in repentance. I learned the concept of God as my HH. I love it. I understood that I had left my first Love and He wanted me back.

What principles, from God's Word (or through our resources), Natasha, did the Lord teach you during this trial?

The absolute number one principle was that He is my Husband and Lover of my soul (Isaiah 54:5–6). It is a revelation that is still refining me. It was there in His word all along but He needed to open my eyes to see it and even now, I am not able to fully wrap my mind around this truth.

The second one is that the man is the head of the woman and Christ is the head of every man (1 Cor. 11:3). I have always been afraid of submitting to a man (childhood issues and societal conditioning), but I have learned that God has called me to submit to His authority and that He is sovereign. "Let every person be in subjection to the governing authorities. For there is no authority except from God, and those which exist are established by God." Romans 13:1. I have learned that whilst I profess to be a Believer, I was a contentious, rebellious wife and that it was by grace that I have been saved. Oh, God helped me through a lot. He is really so good.

What were the most difficult times that God helped you through Natasha?

During the early days of my pregnancy, I unknowingly took a live vaccine because I didn't know that I was pregnant. When I discovered I was pregnant, I had to consider the *teratogenic risk involved and because I was less than 6 weeks pregnant at the time, I could easily have had an abortion (which my husband felt I should do) but I just couldn't have an abortion.

teratogenic is an agent that can disturb the development of the baby. Teratogens halt the pregnancy or produce a congenital malformation (a birth defect).

So, I was like I will just have to deal with it even if this child is not healthy. It was in the middle of this ordeal that my husband left me. At the time, I did not know if I was going to having a healthy child but I remembered telling God that He should please just give me a healthy baby, if He did, I wouldn't mind losing my marriage.

I did a couple of tests to check for any abnormalities (at this time EH was not talking to me). I remembered at about 6 -10 weeks, I had gone for the dating scan. I didn't do the scan to find out the gender, while before the pregnancy, I would have wanted a boy at this time. Yet, I had bigger fish to fry due to the live vaccine, so knowing the gender was no longer an issue or a thought to me. Nonetheless, out of nowhere the sonographer stated that I think this is a boy. You see, I have desired and told God that I would love a boy if I had another child, so when the sonographer told me without me asking that it was going to be a boy, that was God giving me a big cuddle. At this time, I did not care about the sex of the child, I was just worried about having a healthy child. Finally, at the five months mark, I got the all clear that the baby was going to be healthy— Praise God!

The other difficult time was when I was about to give birth. You see, I have other children and we live far from my family. My children were worried about not having their father and mother with them when I left to go to the hospital to give birth.

I had been conversing with my HH about this and oh my, He showed forth amazingly. I got to the hospital and had the baby only two hours later and honestly, both the midwives and I were shocked when the baby popped out. I had just been checked and told I was 4cm dilated, the nurses were getting my paperwork and getting my room organised when I had this incredible urge to push (the very first push). I know not to push until I was well dilated. So I thought I was passing feces but it was my son. I was shocked.

Later I called a family friend to tell her that I have had the baby. She could not believe it, she asked me if it was me she saw driving my car just two hours earlier (unbeknown to me, she had seen my car in traffic two hours earlier).

Tell us HOW it happened Natasha? Did your husband just walk in the front door?

During the times we lived apart, my EH used to visit the kids every Sunday. I was registered to attend a course and emailed hubby asking if he could stay with the older kids whilst I was away. I got no answer back from him. When he eventually answered, it was after the registration date had closed and I emailed him back saying that he should not worry anymore as I had missed that course and would attend the next one.

Even though I said not to bother, my EH showed up on the date I was supposed to attend the course saying that he was here to take care of the kids. And again, I explained that I had sent him an email that I was no longer going but he stayed and never left. Since that day he has been in our house back as if nothing had happened.

Natasha, did you suspect or could you tell you were close to being restored?

No, I did not know he would move back in, not until the day he arrived and didn't leave. I have chosen to be obedient and submit this RMT because my EH has returned home, but you will see from my RMT that things have become more difficult in the physical and the relationship is far from ideal.

Yet, this is what's told to us from the beginning of our courses, that once restoration happens it's not the end of our journey.

So thank you for asking me to submit my testimony because it helped me look back and see how far God has brought us. I know God brought my husband back because, at a point, I was asking God to bring him back only if it was His will. I know that God is Who started the work and He will bring it to completion.

I'd also like to say that God took care of my finances, even though EH said he would not pay the bills. While he was gone he paid the children school fees and took care of our mortgage.

Would you recommend any of our resource in particular that helped you Natasha?

Definitely, all the resources are very important. Reading the Bible, *How God Can and Will Restore Your Marriage*, *By the Word of Their Testimonies* and the online courses. The principle of letting go is very important, when my husband began to visit the children, I knew to stay away. He started complaining to family members that I was refusing to come downstairs to greet him. I needed to let go for my own wellbeing as well. I don't like rejection at all.

Do you have favorite Bible verses that you would like to pass on to women reading your Testimonies? Promises that He gave you?

Isaiah 54:1-8 KJV "Sing, O barren, thou that didst not bear; break forth into singing, and cry aloud, thou that didst not travail with child: for more are the children of the desolate than the children of the married wife, saith the Lord. Enlarge the place of thy tent, and let them stretch forth the curtains of thine habitations: spare not, lengthen thy cords, and strengthen thy stakes; For thou shalt break forth on the right hand and on the left; and thy seed shall inherit the Gentiles, and make the desolate cities to be inhabited. Fear not; for thou shalt not be ashamed: neither be thou confounded; for thou shalt not be put to shame: for thou shalt forget the shame of thy youth, and shalt not remember the reproach of thy widowhood any more. For thy Maker is thine husband; the Lord of hosts is his name; and thy Redeemer the Holy One of Israel; The God of the whole earth shall he be called. For the Lord hath called thee as a woman forsaken and grieved in spirit, and a wife of youth, when thou wast refused, saith thy God. For a small moment have I forsaken thee; but with great mercies will I gather thee. In a little wrath I hid my face from thee for a moment; but with everlasting kindness will I have mercy on thee, saith the Lord thy Redeemer."

Philemon 15-18 KJV "For perhaps he therefore departed for a season, that thou shouldest receive him forever; Not now as a servant, but above a servant, a brother beloved, especially to me, but how much more unto thee, both in the flesh, and in the Lord? If thou count me therefore a partner, receive him as myself. If he hath wronged thee, or oweth thee ought, put that on mine account."

John 10:27 KJV "My sheep hear my voice, and I know them, and they follow me..."

Psalm 17:4 KJV "Concerning the works of men, by the word of thy lips I have kept me from the paths of the destroyer."

Habakkuk 2:2-3 KJV "And the Lord answered me, and said, write the vision, and make it plain upon tables, that he may run that readeth it. For the vision is yet for an appointed time, but at the end it shall speak, and not lie: though it tarry, wait for it; because it will surely come, it will not tarry."

Psalm 37:8 KJV "Cease from anger, and forsake wrath: fret not thyself in any wise to do evil."

Isaiah 55:8-9 KJV "For my thoughts are not your thoughts, neither are your ways my ways, saith the Lord. For as the heavens are higher than the earth, so are my ways higher than your ways, and my thoughts than your thoughts."

Would you be interested in helping encourage other women Natasha?

Yes, I will love to comfort others with the comfort I have gotten from his words and this ministry.

Either way Natasha, what kind of encouragement would you like to leave women with, in conclusion?

God has got this (you and your marriage), TRUST Him. If you know this truth, this journey will be more peaceful and restful. I think one of the things this journey teaches us is that He is super loving and a Husband. GOD is very powerful too and He LOVES YOU, He is working out the details of your life. Let go of your fears, He is the best thing that can happen to you.

You know when He called Peter to get on the waters, He is doing the same today, CALLING you. Keep your eyes on His (His words, lessons from this ministry) and your marriage restoration is a certainty. But what is more beautiful is you being restored to your Groom, your Husband.

Chapter 23

Meggie Ann

"And I will give you a new heart,
and a new spirit I will put within you."
—Ezekiel 36:26

"It's Not About Your Marriage"

Meggy Ann, how did your restoration actually begin?

A woman from my church showed me RMI one day and told me how it helped restore her friend and so many others. I even got a hope card a few months before not even knowing what was to come. I began submitting to the Lord and I found my true Love. I then stopped being a contentious woman and was able to let go of bitterness and forgive. I also let go of my marriage and husband and just gave them to God. It's when I got out of the way and put my all in the Lord, that's when He began changing my husband and me both.

How did God change your situation as you sought Him wholeheartedly Meggy Ann?

First God worked on me, He softened my heart, He began showing me I was a contentious woman filled with bitterness and unforgiveness. He began changing me and drawing me closer to Him. He broke my chains and gave me a gentle and quiet spirit. When I became kind and loving, I was no longer trying to control or condemn my husband. That's when he started to visit my daughters and soon he wanted to see me more as well. He was kind and we didn't fight since I put my all in Him. I didn't have to pressure my EH for things because I knew my HH had it. That caused the hate wall that my husband had put up, begin to crumble before me as he became kind and open. He started showing me affection and now says I love you again. Since I have my first love, my HH, I knew I am loved and didn't feel the need to force him to say it to me.

What principles, from God's Word (or through our resources), Meggy Ann, did the Lord teach you during this trial?

I was a contentious woman. It was all about me. Truth is, he wasn't this horrible bad guy. I was the one who needed to change, a lot. I was just as much to blame for what happened in our marriage. I needed to be reconciled to my first Love, my HH. He is and will always be first in my life from now on! I need Him. I learned that He is always enough and I need to bring everything to Him, even my tears. I needed a gentle and quiet spirit. And my EH could be won without a word from me. Also how my home needed to be a place of peace and how I needed to raise up my children do the hard things in life.

Meggy Ann, what were the most difficult times that God helped you through?

When I wouldn't hear from my EH for days or weeks it was difficult. Or, if he would say something really hurtful. When he would ignore me or tell me he didn't want me; he didn't care about me and our marriage wasn't worth it. I now know it was all lies that satan was feeding him to say.

What was the "turning point" of your restoration Meggy Ann?

When I fully let go of my marriage and husband and clung to my HH. Once I put Him first I no longer hurt so much—I felt more peace and joy. I wanted only Him. He was and is enough. I stopped trying to control the situation, I shut my mouth prayed, fasted and was kind and loving no matter what.

Tell us HOW it happened Meggy Ann? Did your husband just walk in the front door?

My husband was asking me what shift at work he should take. I told him as long as he was able to see our daughters it didn't matter to me but he kept asking. Then he started saying *hypothetically* "if we got back together what would I like" so I told him. The very next day he comes to the house and tells me he's going to get that shift and asked me if he got a new place for him, the girls and for me, would I live with him? I said it might be hard with everything going on, then he told me he wants our marriage and wants us to live together as a family and that he called off the separation.

The next day we went to his grandparents who mean the world to him to tell them we are back together for good. He also said he is giving up drinking, he told me I am the only woman he has ever loved and wants to have a long life with. He told me he wants to be the type of man his girls should look for to marry—a man who loves his wife and the Lord and doesn't just walk away when it gets hard. He said he wants to start going to church. I'm in shock but I'm trusting the Lord who will take care of everything.

Meggy Ann, did you suspect or could you tell you were close to being restored?

I asked the Lord for hope when I thought I just couldn't take it anymore. Then my close friend showed up to talk to me. She lives in Indiana, not close to me, but her adult daughter lives here. She has a restored marriage and always encouraged me to keep my eyes on my first Love not on my husband. When I saw her it was like the Lord was saying "Are you ready?" Everyone I ran into kept telling me to wait, don't give up, then a couple days later my husband returned. It's funny cause I'd fully let go of my marriage and my husband. I was truly happy with just me and my girls and the Lord, but I started feeling like it was gonna happen. Then things also got even harder as everyone said they would, so I knew.

Would you recommend any of our resource Meggy Ann that helped you?

The courses were amazing! I had no money but was able to do them!! It completely changed me. I had God's Word everyday fed to me and reading "Psalms" and "Proverbs" was wonderful too. I still read everything everyday.

Do you have favorite Bible verses that you would like to pass on to women reading your Testimonies? Promises that He gave you Meggy Ann?

Psalm 37:5
Commit your way to the Lord; trust in him and he will do this.

James 4:10
Humble yourselves before the Lord, and he will lift you up.

Proverbs 16:7
When a man's ways please the Lord, he makes even his enemies to be at peace with him.

Romans 12:21
Do not be overcome with evil but overcome evil with good.

Meggy Ann, would you be interested in helping encourage other women?

Yes

What kind of encouragement would you like to leave women with, in conclusion Meggy Ann?

Give everything to Lord. Let go and be with your first Love. Put your all in Him so you can discover what real love is. Look to see Him at your side and listen to the changes the Lord wants to make in you. Let go of your marriage and your husband give everything to our Lord. Step out of the way and let God work. Also don't try to be your husband holy spirit. This is a spiritual war; **it's not about your marriage**. Trust the Lord and hope against hope. Cling to the Lord, He is your HH.

Chapter 24

Valentina

"Wait for the Lord; be strong,
and let your heart take courage."
—Psalm 27:14

"Restored Even After Husband Moved to Another Country"

Valentina, how did your restoration actually begin?

My journey began in 2012 and it was all of a sudden. I found the RMI a few months after my husband left home. I was devastated, I had gotten to the bottom of the well. But now I know it was necessary for me to have a broken heart so that the good seed could be planted in my life. Since then, my mind has been renewed daily by God, through the resources of the RMI and daily encouragement.

How did God change your situation Valentina as you sought Him wholeheartedly?

I was totally impatient, anxious, independent, proud, vain, lying to my husband and not submissive to him. I did not respect my mother or any authorities God placed in my life. I lived for the world and God was not first in my heart. I believed in God, but I was so far away from Him!

First God showed me all the wrong paths I had taken in my life, all wrong decisions I had made. Then He began to teach me many importants things. I learned the importance of submission. I learned to have a gentle and quiet spirit, not to gossip and to exhibit self-control. I began to win others without words and to leave everything in God's hand, trusting He would answer me at just the right time.

I began to ask for His guidance in all decisions I had to make. I waited patiently. I began to pray and intercede for other people. I began to forgive and pray for those who hurt me. He helped me to not be unhappy and hurt when people gossip about my situation, because I knew in my heart my God is greater, nothing is impossible with God and He is always by my side. I learned to be humble, patient and trustworthy. God became first in my life and I fell madly in love with Him, my Lord and Savior. Now I see Him as my God, my Savior, my Lovely Husband! He is everything to me!!!

What principles, from God's Word (or through our resources), Valentina, did the Lord teach you during this trial?

Principle 1: Do not get lost - the ONLY way we can get to our destination, our restoration, is by holding our HH's hand. How important it is to have the Lord, our God, as first in our lives and this will only happen if we invest in our relationship with Him. I made a commitment to God during my journey: I would wake up early and read His word and meditate on the verses that He used to touch my heart. I fasted on TV and spent more time with Him, my Beloved. And every time I thought of my husband or my marriage, I read the verses that He gave me that day.

Principle 2: Lighten your luggage - You need to Let go. This principle is the most difficult and also one of the most important. We should practice it EVERY DAY too. Placing everything into the hands of God, not just our husband and our marriage, but EVERYTHING. I left everything in His hands. Anything that came to my mind to worry or make me anxious, I immediately surrendered to His hands and asked Him to help me let go and trust Him. I repeated that God has great things for my family and that I and my family will serve the Lord.

This journey was used by God to change me and mold me according to His will. And He has done a great job on me, but there is still so much to do. So I'm going to focus on the verses that show me how to behave and trust Him to guide me to be the woman He wants me to be.

Principle 3: Freedom will set you free. "Now faith is the assurance of things hoped for, and the evidence of things which we do not see." Hebrews 11: 1. How wonderful is to read the word of God and to have our mind renewed by His truth. It's Liberating!!!

What were the most difficult times that God helped you through Valentina?

At the beginning of my journey I acted on my own understanding, being disobedient to God, and got to the bottom of the well. But God is merciful and that's when He reached out and took care of me, giving me strength and teaching me His truths. After a year and a half, when my relationship with the Lord was more mature and deeper, problems at work began to spring up, but the more they appeared, the more I clung to the Lord and it was when I found myself completely in love with Him and felt my heart burst again with joy and love.

Valentina, what was the "turning point" of your restoration?

When I was able to understand the principle of "letting go" and put everything into God's hands. I began to trust Him completely, I lived in peace, without worrying when, how and if my marriage would be restored. I also went to work for this ministry, doing things for God and with Him to help other women.

In September of 2013, I wrote a Praise Report that I never sent on purpose, because it was a report of praise — thanking Him for all the changes God was making in my life and believing that I would soon be writing my Restored Marriage Testimony. I did this because He had guided me to write the praise report but not to send it. At the end of the PR I even wrote the title of my testimony: RESTORED EVEN AFTER THE HUSBAND MOVED TO ANOTHER COUNTRY. :) God is wonderful

Tell us HOW it happened Valentina? Did your husband just walk in the front door? Valentina, did you suspect or could you tell you were close to being restored?

After the new year, my husband contacted me. We always talked on the internet because he was living in the USA. After we talked, he complained that he was in US for seven months and I had never visited him. I said if he wanted me to go for a visit I would do it. He then said he had already called me to come but I had declined. That's when I realized that I had been disobedient to him (the first time he invited me) and had been disobedient to God too.

So I asked God's forgiveness for not being submissive. Then I told my husband that I would go to US to visit him, since I would be on an extended vacation from work. He told me to come, but to come only as a friend. I spent the month of January preparing for the trip, fasting for favor and asking God for guidance. I arrived in the USA on February 1 and this was the same day that my marriage was restored by God— when my husband told me that he wanted to stay with me, but he did not want me to make any sacrifice for him. That's when I said that I loved him and that I would gladly leave my job to stay with him, supporting him in whatever he needed, because he was my husband. I told him all this always praying silently, asking God for guidance and trusting in His promises.

Would you recommend any of our resource in particular that helped you Valentina?

I recommend all the courses available, and not just do it once, but do as many times as the Lord directs you to do. I did each of them more than twice and every time I did, the Holy Spirit convicted me about new things. *How God Can and Will Restore Your Marriage* also *A Wise Woman*. All of the *By the Word of Their Testimonies*, and going through online courses.

Would you be interested in helping encourage other women Valentina?

Yes, always! I am already part of the ministry team.

Either way Valentina, what kind of encouragement would you like to leave women with, in conclusion?

Wake up early and spend time with your Heavenly Husband. Speak to the Lord about everything. Spend more time with Him throughout the day, especially meditating on His Word. Fast regularly. Stop watching television for a while, especially romantic movies since they are a stumbling block to restoration. Listen to praise music and read the Word of God. Praise Him even (principally) in difficult times. Pray for other people but stop praying asking for restoration. Let go. Take the RMI courses and read the books over and over again, until the principles are set firmly in your heart.

~ Valentina in Brazil, RESTORED

On February 5, 2018 the Lord, Valentina's HH, called...

Our sweet bride Valentina is no longer with us, but is now with her HH. "Let us rejoice and be glad and give him glory! For the wedding of the Lamb has come, and His bride has made herself ready."
Revelation 19:7

When Valentina first came to restore her marriage, she began by volunteering and was soon our Portuguese RESTORED Marriage Minister.

For many years Valentina helped make the Portuguese ministry what it is today.

Valentina specialized in being a successful professional woman, an architect, was raised Catholic, and had a husband who believed we "deserve" better as the reason for him asking for separation when he first left her in 2012.

Once restored, Valentina took an extended sabbatical soon after He called several others to take her place. When we called her back, we believe she returned so we could help make her ready for her wedding day with Him. We are so thankful we got to know and love Valentina for all these years. She will remain an inspiration and be missed by us all.

Chapter 25

Lizzy

"For still the vision,
awaits its appointed time."
—Habakkuk 2:3

"Too Late!!"

Dear RMI. I'm writing to thank you and let you know that this is the best Thanksgiving I've ever had. Two months ago, I called my closest friend desperate to know what to do. Another one of our friends had just called me to tell me that she was planning to divorce her husband. So, I called my closest friend to see if someone would be willing to talk some sense into her before she made the biggest mistake of her life. The friend I called had a restored marriage but hers was the only one who's had a happy ending, or should I say a new beginning. So many of our friends were divorcing and I just wanted each of our friends to know that divorce was not the answer. So, I called and asked that my friend call our mutual friend to talk some sense into her!

Let me explain that both our friend and her husband are Christians. So, no one could understand what went wrong. After my restored friend got home from going to see our friend she called me back. She said, "Nothing was really wrong" that our girlfriend said she just felt that God had released her from her marriage! She said she just no longer felt that she "wanted" to be married anymore, and since they had no children, she felt God said she could leave.

So, then I called her myself and read a few things to her from *How God Will Restore Your Marriage*. I told her flat out that she had been deceived into thinking that God had released her from her marriage. I told her His Word clearly says that "He hates divorce" and that "He is the same yesterday, today and tomorrow." I also explained that many times Satan comes to us as an "angel of light" in order to deceive us, and that very often he even uses scripture from the bible just as he did with Jesus in the desert to destroy lives. That it was the enemy who was telling her she was released from her marriage and he was going to destroy her life if she didn't stop what was about to happen.

I know it was God when I began to share a bunch of "what if" scenarios. Like, "what if" later she found that she had made a huge mistake and that she wanted her husband back, but he had found someone else? Unfortunately, nothing I said made any difference. She was going through with the divorce at that was it!! Nothing I said, no matter how many good points I made could persuade her to stop pushing for the divorce. She said (almost like it wasn't the same friend I knew because she was so cold) that she was not interested in any "principles" and that she **knew** that she was released and asked that I not bother her again! I confess that I hung up fuming!

So, fast forward about a year, and I heard that my friend did regret what she'd done. She knew she had made a mistake in leaving her husband. Another friend told me she heard she wanted her husband to come back and was trying to get back together with him. But all of us knew that about 2 months after they separated, her husband had met someone else. So our friend demanded their pastor call her ex husband and force him to work on their marriage. Her husband refused and then about two or three months later he married the other woman.

So, I know this doesn't sound like a happy ending, but God did bring more calamity into our friend's life. After her husband remarried, our friend got breast cancer. Though it sounds horrible it's almost like it's what our friend needed. It broke her like nothing else could. A month or so later I thought I had seen her at the mall shopping, holding hands with her ex husband. I texted my restored friend because I just knew it had to be her!

What my restored friend told me was such a shock. It seems that our friend still had your book How God Will Restore Your Marriage we gave her way back when she didn't want us to bother her. And one night she just began reading it. Even though she was the one who'd done everything wrong (for such selfish reasons too), she believed God could still restore her marriage. She asked God to change her and He did.

God also made sure that her ex husband's marriage didn't last long at all, I believe it was only a few months when his new wife cheated on him and left him. So, the last chapter (that God always loves to write) is that when I saw them in the mall they'd already remarried. Our friend's health is also good, so I was wrong when I told my restored friend it was too late.

Our friend ~ Lizzy in South Dakota, is now RESTORED and healthy

Chapter 26

Valerie

"The king's heart is like
channels of water in the hand
of the LORD; He turns it
wherever He wishes."
—Proverbs 21:1

"Today My Husband is a Dedicated Father"

What brought you to RMI? Please use this space to briefly let our readers know what your life was like when you first found us, Valerie, so our readers understand just what a miracle your restoration is.

Valerie, how did your restoration actually begin?

Today I am here writing my dream testimony, in fact, I could have written it before, but I confess that I was afraid because I was still very lost after my restoration. Until I received a study from RMI that alerted me how important submitting a restored testimony was (even if things weren't perfect) in order to move forward with my journey now that I'm restored. Then because I still hadn't submitted it, I heard from a very dear sister who confirmed to me that God wanted me to write His praise. So now I realize that I failed to give the honor to the One who is worthy to receive the honor and the praise for what He's done for me! And once I did, everything began to change and become better.

Yes, there were trials, but as I put Him first, as I remained close to my HH, everything began to move forward again. But I'm getting ahead of myself.

So, it all started in August more than 7 years ago. I decided to accept a marriage proposal from my daughter's father. We had a beautiful ceremony, a wonderful wedding reception, and we were sure we would be very happy—living happily ever after.

How did God change your situation Valerie as you sought Him wholeheartedly?

But like so many marriages, as soon as we got home and were alone, just ourselves, something started to change. I was always very jealous and contentious, in fact, I had not forgiven the mistakes from my husband's past. My jealousy was possessive, I fought with him about everything. I always wanted to rule over everything and make all the decisions. My husband could not be the man of the house because I— I was already doing his part and I only began recognizing it when I got to the bottom of the pit. In fact, the turning point was when I found the book *How God Can and Will Restore Your Marriage* and my eyes opened to all my mistakes and it was then that I started to change.

What principles, from God's Word (or through our resources), Valerie, did the Lord teach you during this trial?

Of course, my husband also had his mistakes, but I learned that a wise woman builds the house and the fool tears it down. How many times did he ask me why I acted like a crazy woman towards him? But it was the way all women acted, I had no idea where I was headed. Yet it was clear my marriage was growing cold, and I did not understand why. After all, we were in the presence of God when we said our vows. We had planned for a future together. But more and more my husband became distant, moving away from me, until one day five years ago, just after celebrating our 2nd wedding anniversary, we had a disgustingly ugly discussion, that turned into a horrible fight, and that's when he said he did not want the marriage anymore. I could not believe it because before we married, so many times, he had said that same thing but always took it back. Not this time, this time it was for real! After a week, he left home, and I did not know where he was. I did not know anything....

Not until I found out that he was with an OW, a "friend" from his work. A woman who had become his confidant, someone he could talk to who would listen and let him be a man. That day, he moved out of our home and in with her.

What were the most difficult times that God helped you through Valerie?

So I began to seek God with more intensity than before. That's when I really knew the Lord personally for the first time in my life. I found Him as my HH after taking a course someone suggested, the Finding the Abundant Life

Course. Before finding Him as my HH, I cried a lot, I suffered a lot, I went through all kinds of humiliation, all because of who I was, but His love began to change me.

What hurt the most was when I saw my little girl suffer so much. To add to that hurt, so many people told me to give up, to live my life, live my life just as my husband had and find someone new. They said I was stupid to think that my husband would ever come back. The enemy would scream in my ear, asking me just how many times I'd heard my husband say that he did not love me anymore, and then say that he was planning to ask me for a divorce? But the Lord told me, He would not allow it and to trust Him.

Over the course of the next year, when I became His bride, my EH began to tell me that "someday" he would come back. But just after giving me that encouragement, he'd disappear again. In truth, my EH came back twice but left again after only a few days. He'd also dropped the first OW but then would quickly get another. Each time I would turn my attention to who was there to love me, my true Husband, and each time I found myself falling more and more in love with Him.

Valerie, what was the "turning point" of your restoration?

Anyway, as I said, each time I let him go without saying a word, and then I started to focus on my relationship with the Lord, my HH and each time I strengthen myself in His truths and by helping minister to other women. But the moment I began helping several women, things got really horrible.

Yet, that was the turning point. At the moment when I really thought I did not want my marriage restored, the moment I ignored what was coming against me, the moment I focused on helping other women. Literally, in a blink of an eye, my husband came back to me with a changed heart! After years of wandering in the desert, my husband said he wanted to try again and that I could trust what he said because he had lost everything. He said he wanted our family to put God first and that he would try to be a good spiritual leader if I would let him. Wow!

Tell us HOW it happened Valerie? Did your husband just walk in the front door? Valerie, did you suspect or could you tell you were close to being restored?

Now you must be thinking why, only now, after almost two years I decided to submit my testimony. It's because I was thinking that everything should be perfectly marvelous, and it was not quite like that. So, I thought I should share my testimony when things were perfect.

I thought, once everything is smooth, the way I thought "restoration was supposed to be" then I would do it. But because my husband still had some struggles because of the enemy's still trying to destroy our lives, maybe even more because everyone was in awe that he was home and faithful to me, the more I reasoned I should wait.

Yes, we had other trials that came at us—but nothing like when it was adultery that was coming against us!

One trial that came that almost took our marriage down, was when I was tempted to undo what God did! At one point I saw myself returning to the contentious, controlling woman I'd been. But thanks to Him, thanks to His love, thanks to my HH, I had the strength to let that woman die. Today I am harvesting what I sowed with such joy!!!

I've helped several women seek restoration and become His bride. My husband says that he loves me, takes with me to church and has strengthened himself in the presence of the Lord. He is truly our spiritual leader. I stopped being contentious and we lived in perfect peace. His relationship with our daughter has improved a lot (she was hurt because he'd introduced so many "new mommies" to her) but today my husband is a dedicated father. They have a newfound love as father and daughter. (I have attached a picture of them at a father daughter dance she invited him to.)

Today I just had to praise the Lord for everything, for He has never forsaken me, never left my side and has given me a love that I am able to pour out on my husband, daughter and so many hurting confused women!

Would you recommend any of our resource in particular that helped you Valerie?

Yes, I recommend the book *How God Can and Will Restore Your Marriage* also *A Wise Woman* book. I recommend taking the online courses and reading the daily encouragement every day.

Would you be interested in helping encourage other women Valerie?

Yes. I have a local ministry for women that helps many continue on their journey to know Him.

Either way Valerie, what kind of encouragement would you like to leave women with, in conclusion?

Remember one thing, "The king's heart is like channels of water in the hand of the LORD; He turns it wherever He wishes." Proverbs 21:1

Chapter 27

Lindsey

"Your word is a lamp for my feet,
a light on my path."
—Psalm 119:105

"My Husband Packed His Bags
and Came Home"

When I discovered RMI and your materials I was very young, and we already had two small boys. We got married because I was pregnant while still in high school. I know my husband always felt trapped, and after he had left me, he told me to move back to my mother's. Not only had my husband left me and our two boys, but I also heard that he was actually living with another woman who had recently had his baby, a family he moved in and why he'd asked me to move out. To say I was devastated doesn't come close to how I felt. Everyone knew and everyone began telling me what to do. I was confused, broken, and it was worse when I looked at my two boys playing knowing that whatever choice I made would affect them for the rest of their lives.

My parents made us all go to Sunday school but I never really knew why I was there to hear the same stories over and over again (which is why I never planned to send my boys). But when my mom offered to take them on Sunday I let her, and while they were gone, I got on my knees and began to ask the Lord for help. The next Sunday my mom asked me to go with them, and I went. Right after the service a couple in my mom's church came up to me and said they were praying for me. That's when they told me that they had a restored marriage and told me about the Restore Ministries resources, and said that they would help me get through this.

They bought the books, and I began to read, then they'd invite me to meet with them regularly to pray. They would never let me talk about anything

having to do with my husband because they said that "God knew th
and we'd "do better to leave all of that with Him." We prayed toget
sometimes praying for specific things, but most often we prayed for His
will. Praying specifically helped at first. After praying for my sons and me
to move back home, my husband called one day and told me I could move
back home, but then I found out it was only because he was moving with
the OW and was moving with her to another state.

It was soon after reading *How God Will Restore Your Marriage* and the
Wise Woman workbook for women, that I began to apply the principles on
fasting with prayer. Not only did this not help, but soon after I added the
fasting, things got much worse the more I prayed and fasted. One morning
when I answered a knock at my door, I was shocked when I saw a sheriff
and was "served with divorce papers." I was shaking when I called to tell
my prayer couple what happened, but they told me fasting with my prayers
was just moving things to a close faster.

What I didn't know was how right they were. I found out later that at the
exact hour in another state, my husband was packing his bags. He was
staying in a motel room, and after he had thrown everything into his
suitcase, he told me later, that he got in his truck. He pulled out and headed
south then came to a fork in the road. He stopped his car in the middle of
the deserted road, and he asked God to steer his truck—either to the right
(which would bring him home) or to the left (which would bring him back
to join the other woman.

All my prayers were answered — the truck pulled abruptly to the RIGHT!

Back at home, instead of falling apart the way I would have before I became
spiritually strong by fasting, I hung up the phone and grabbed the D papers
in my hand, grabbed my keys and drove over to the couple's house to pray.
The three of us stood together with the D papers on the floor. We held hands
and prayed together against those divorce papers using dozens of Bible
verses letting them do the talking and what they were meant to do.

Four hours later I was at home when my husband's truck pulled into the
driveway. I saw him pull his red suitcase from the back of the truck and
walked to the front door as I threw it open. We were hugging each other
when our boys' school bus pulled up, and they came running up to us. To
say that was the happiest day of my life can't describe how I felt then, and
now when I look back. I'm only sorry I didn't share my story sooner so it
could help women who may be facing things like what I had to go through.

Once my husband was settled down being back at home, I knew it was time for me to talk to my husband, telling him about my prayers, how I'd fasted, and most importantly about my new relationship with the Lord. I explained I had become a Christian while he was gone and I began to share my faith with him. He didn't say much, but I left the details with the Lord. I didn't want what happened to be a secret, and I knew that my husband needed the Lord just as much as I did back when I discovered Him. By coming back to me he'd lost his job, so this was a perfect time for me to help him like that couple had helped me.

The following Sunday, my husband was dressed before I got up, sitting at the table with an old bible placed next to his coffee. So we all hurried and dressed and went to the Sunday service, and right after the end of the service, my husband went to the altar himself and accepted the Lord. That night our pastor asked us if we'd be willing to share our testimony and I was surprised when my husband said yes. That night we each told our half of the story with our very huge church congregation. About a month later, my husband asked me if I'd renew our wedding vows, which we also did in the Sunday evening service.

About a year later I met the couple again and told them I was on a prolonged 30 day fast. I told them that the Lord had impressed upon my heart to adopt my husband's baby girl. We had heard that the baby had been left for months with friends of ours while the other woman went overseas after joining the service. What we heard and what everyone was saying is that she had "lost interest in her daughter soon after her lover had gone back to his wife." My hope and prayer are that God will do a miracle and we can adopt my husband's little girl.

Due to medical issues (I'd had an abortion after my sons without telling my husband) that left me unable to have children again. God had forgiven me, and I felt this was the girl I'd always dreamed I'd have some day.

~ Lindsey in Florida, RESTORED

UPDATE: We heard from this older prayer couple that they were able to adopt the little girl and who looks just like her two brothers. And whenever anyone comments how much they look alike, Lindsey loves to share the testimony of who she is as an opportunity to share the Lord with people. What they are amazed the most about is how she explains how they encourage her "real mom" to visit and how they were able (as a couple) to share the Lord with her and she'd given her heart to the Lord!

Chapter 28

Tanya

"And He will make your paths straight."
—Proverbs 3:5

"One Step Forward and Two Steps Back"

What brought you to RMI? Please use this space to briefly let our readers know what your life was like when you first found us, Tanya, so our readers understand just what a miracle your restoration is.

Tanya, how did your restoration actually begin?

I knew that my marriage was no longer the same as it had been, and I became concerned. The fights were constant, and they were over really small things. Each time we fought, I could sense my husband was moving away from me emotionally. I realized he was avoiding me, as if I had become an unwelcome and unpleasant person to be around. When I walked towards him, he walked away. He seemed to be running away from me. This was troubling because we have always been very passionate, perfect partners and close friends. He never did anything without me, which after a while I started to complain about, because even when I'd go to another aisle to buy a soap in the market, he followed me.

After only 3 years of being married, something broke between us.

It happened one very sad Saturday when he had gone out with my brother-in-law and left his cell phone at home. I looked through everything I could and then found something that caused me to become jealous. So, like everyone, I confronted him as soon as he arrived home. After our "discussion" I remember him walking away, telling me that he did not love me anymore and he saw me as "just a friend." When he said that, I stormed out of the room, I packed up my things and said, "We're done, it's over!" and we are over!!

That night I spent at my parents' house and the next day he begged me to come back, saying that I did not have to stay 10 minutes away from him. He said he wanted me to know that he still loved me. So, I went home, but we stayed like this, two friends living together, until the cycle started all over again.

One day, after he'd spent all day rejecting my company, I called him "to talk" and try to understand his motives. He told me, crying, that I had been the best thing that had happened in his life, but he could not explain to me what he was feeling—that he rejected me without knowing or understanding it. I broke into a desperate cry, as if my life had ended at that moment. Though this time I did not leave the house.

That same day, before I slept, I had asked the Lord for help. While falling asleep I began to sense what He was showing me. He was showing me that I had not returned to Him. I had not shown Him the love He wanted to have with me. Having a sincerity of heart that I longed for in my husband, I no longer longed for the Lord in the same way. Not for a very long time.

When I woke up, I was still feeling disoriented. Asking Him to show me, He led me to do a Google search for something that could help me find Him the way I needed Him to be in my life. I remember that the very first link that appeared to me was the RMI website and then I discovered the book *How God Can and Will Restore Your Marriage*.

How did God change your situation Tanya as you sought Him wholeheartedly?

As soon as I discovered Erin's book, I read it in two days and felt so much closer to the Lord. I began to apply the principles and my husband began noticing that I was becoming quieter and quieter, more peaceful. I recognized my past mistakes and took them to heart. I had always been contentious, I wanted everything to be my way. I was impulsive and impatient, and I realized that my husband often agreed with what I said so as not to get into a discussion or fight.

I asked the Lord for forgiveness and I began to create a greater intimacy with Him. My journey in the desert began in November and I understood what God wanted to do in me. But as soon as the trials started, I went back to who I was, contentious and I failed to strengthen myself in the Lord.

The enemy continued with his schemes, doing everything to cause me to stumble, because I was weak in faith. Those were very difficult months, the worst months of my life. My husband became more and more distant once I changed back to who I'd been. He became a total stranger to me, a completely indifferent man. To cope, he began drinking more than socially, spending hours in the gym, and packed his life full of things to occupy his mind and stay away from me. I felt horrible and instead of seeking the Lord and remaining steadfastly in His love, I questioned my husband and demanded answers. I was sarcastic, which further distanced him from me. But in spite of everything I knew the right thing to do, according to the principles of the book, but sadly I did not follow them. I was now aware that I was not pleasing to God. Each day I took one step forward and two steps back.

What principles, from God's Word (or through our resources), Tanya, did the Lord teach you during this trial?

Basically, all the principles I've learned have been proven to be true based on my experiences. These principles really work, but only if we apply them. Whenever I did anything His way, God always confirmed to me by so much positive reaction from my husband and I felt at peace. When I did things my way, the world's way, the popular way, it caused me grief and unraveled what He'd done.

What were the most difficult times that God helped you through Tanya?

After I realized that I knew the right thing to do and did not do it, my spirit began to really bother me, deeply convicting me. Many things that Erin mentioned in her book that would happen, happened. Relatives told me that if he did not love me anymore, it was best to move on and that it did not look like he was ever going to change. They said so many discouraging things. It was then that I felt that I had to follow the principles. I truly realized it was my fault that my situation had not changed. I had delayed doing what was right. I was a lukewarm Christian.

That day a very great force took hold of my heart and I knew that I must be firm in my obedience because everything depended on me. I had pulled my house down, over and over again, and I had to be who I needed to be, or it would be over.

I've been blessed to have a dear friend, Tara, who is a true woman of God and a great intercessor. A lot that my husband did she did not understand, mostly because I saw myself as a victim, and it's the way I often described myself to her. So, God sent Tara to be part of a powerful three-strand cord and I believe that He loved her so much that He wanted to teach her how to see things. Tara never married, nor does she have or want children. But she has an incredible heart. I knew for Tara to help me, especially to intercede for me correctly, I had to give her the book to read. Even though she was a passionate Christian who knows her Bible, she had never seen things from Erin's point of view. She was astonished and immediately asked me for forgiveness, and also asked God, for all the wrong advice she had given me and so many others who'd come to her for help. Although she had always been by my side, from the first time I foolishly left the house until the last. Once she finished reading the book, I knew I had someone by my side who was like-minded and knew the truth.

Holding me accountable to the lessons, I began by fasting from Facebook, since it was something that took my time. Time I now wanted to dedicate to becoming more intimate with the Lord.

As confirmation that I was to go forward in this purpose, the day I made this decision, my husband became restless and called me to talk. He apologized for everything, for not giving me a hand when he knew I needed help. He apologized for not coming near me and ignoring me. He said he knew he was not acting like we were a couple, but again said he did not understand what was happening inside him. He told me there was a void, an emptiness he couldn't explain. He said that there was no OW (and thankfully there was not) but if that were the case it would be easier for him to explain it. He felt there was no explanation. It was something that made him want to disappear from me and life…

I said nothing. A single tear streamed down my face and I could only respond by saying, "Do not worry about me, I will not do anything foolish. I promise, I'll be fine." I left to get ready to go to church, where I poured my heart out, crying rivers of tears to the Lord. I gave everything into the hands of God and asked Him for two things: that my husband would not take his ring off his finger and that he continue to respect me by remaining faithful. That night I went to sleep without eating anything and I clung to the Lord with all my might.

I always took my worries to God so that was not new. But that night I tried my best to let my husband go, even though we still lived and slept together. To let go in my situation, since we were sleeping and waking up together, was something extremely complicated for me. But the Lord helped me in everything. I always brought my concerns to Him, so I knew He would speak to my husband and he would remain faithful to our marriage, according to His will. The more I let go, the more I sought intimacy with the Lord, the more I saw him pursuing me.

Tanya, what was the "turning point" of your restoration?

I know that the moment I came nearer to the Lord, the enemy rose up strongly against me.

The turning point was when I discovered my husband's involvement with a co-worker. Although he did not demonstrate the existence of OW, because he always came home at regular hours and behaved in the same way he had always behaved, I had no idea. And yet, because of my HH I was already properly prepared by the Lord to deal with this situation.

Tell us HOW it happened Tanya? Did your husband just walk in the front door? Tanya, did you suspect or could you tell you were close to being restored?

One day I had a dream that he had betrayed me. I woke up very distressed and asked the Lord to get rid of it, but that if it was of His will, I would accept whatever came to me and I knew that He would give me the strength to bear it.

Since the day, somewhere in the middle of my journey, I had discovered pornography on his cell phone, which is why we had the huge discussion (that I mentioned early). He had changed the password, so I would not get in, but it didn't matter. In fact, I did not even want to snoop anymore because I was afraid of what I might see. But the very next week I already knew the new password. But as I said, I didn't use it nor did I tell anyone I knew it. After all, I did not want to tell someone I knew the password, because I knew the enemy would begin to tempt me and I'd make a fatal move. I spent months without even wanting to get near his cell phone.

The turning point happened after a party, when at two in the morning, while we were in bed sleeping, the phone rang with a message on his WhatsApp. I woke up and asked who was sending him a message at that time of the morning. He was drowsy and upset at having been woken up, he said did not know who it was. Then he said that it was probably just a drunk friend. But because I was tired, I kept insisting, which made him get upset. He picked up his pillow and went to sleep on the living room sofa.

Unfortunately, he did not take the cell phone because he was certain that I did not know the password. Foolishly, as soon as he left, I picked up the cell phone, I logged in and saw a loving message from the OW. As much as it had hurt me, hurt too much to bare, I remained quiet. A few minutes later he came back and saw the look of pain on my face. He knew I'd seen it.

Though I would have normally gone off in a rage or cried my eyes out, there was not even a tear on my face! I knew God was with me, holding me and comforting me. I said nothing, just looked into my husband's eyes. I finally had a gentle and quiet spirit due only to His love.

He apologized to me and said that the enemy was trying to confuse and mess with his feelings. It was very difficult for both of us, not just me. He left the room, and only then did I cry at the Lord's feet. I barely slept. I confess that I know I should have stayed, but the next morning I packed some things to spend a few days at my parents' house. He asked me lovingly to stay, but he knew I had to go and get away.

As soon as I got there, I sent him a message saying that I knew I needed to forgive him but living with him would be more difficult now that I knew.

I turned my focus towards asking my HH to help me find the forgiveness He had put inside of me. I poured myself out to the Lord. I deleted all my social networks and WhatsApp and told God I wanted to let my husband go, so HE would live in me and that my husband could live the way he wanted to live. I gave it all into the hands of God.

Immediately my husband started to look for me when he saw I had shut down my social networks. He called me a couple of times that day to find out how I was and sent several SMS messages.

Very soon I began to feel compassion and I was able to release His forgiveness towards him and the OW. God started to turn my heart towards him and his heart back to me. Once he called me from work to find out how I was, he said he missed me, that it was stupid what he did. I was able to tell him I did forgive him, that I knew he did not try to hurt me, and that I also forgave the OW. He said he was amazed at my behavior, my calmness and thanked me for forgiving him. He said that I am very strong and that I was very different.

I spent two weeks at my parents' house. Soon after he sent me an SMS saying that he always loved me, when I remembered the testimony of Dan, and also Sue's husband. In that time, we began to meet and speak to each other just like we were boyfriend and girlfriend, flirty and sweet to each other. In one of our conversations, he told me that the fact that I had forgiven him, really attracted him to me. I remembered immediately that Erin had written this in her book, and that forgiveness was appealing.

In those distant days, when I was too broken to move, I saw my husband begin seeking the Lord, hearing praises from him daily, and he said for the first time in his life he enjoyed and looked forward to reading the Bible.

Anyway, he asked me to come home and I knew it was time. When I arrived, he asked me to be patient with him, because he was still shaken by everything.

All this 'turning point' happened coincidentally when I started receiving the weekly encouragements on 'Are you really ready?' for restoration!!" Erin, you helped me IMMENSELY to understand everything that happened and is still happening now!! It's been almost two months since I came home and we're living with a mix of feelings.

He began to call me affectionate nicknames, as he had done before. He wants to be by my side again and we have sensed a tight bond between us. But I still see an inner struggle within him. His cell phone no longer has a blocking password because he wants to be open and transparent. And what the enemy still uses to try to steal my peace, is that OW still works with him. But he's told me that he cut off relations with her, never even speaks to her in any way. I know how difficult it has to be for him, so I cannot do anything but praise and thank God for the wonderful works that He has wrought on our behalf.

Yes, as Erin tells us all the time, the return is hard and difficult, which is why we need to put HIM first in our heart and why He has our restoration journey so difficult to prepare us for restoration. I know that God will continue to orchestrate everything and finish the work that He began in us.

What I can say happened that is important to emphasize is this: the week after my return home, after a nightmare I had about my husband and OW, I woke up with an immense desire to fast. At first, it was for the purpose of breaking any connection between the two of them, but then on the third day, God showed me that He wanted to talk to me, so I could hear Him clearly during my fast.

So, on the third day the Lord spoke, and He warned me that I was again being unfaithful to Him! I was not putting Him first. He said I was again turning away from my first Love. He gave me a verse from the book of Jeremiah that made it very clear and it says: in Psalms "For they triggered

His wrath by setting up high places, altars to god's in His land; they aroused His jealousy by bowing down to idols in the shadow of His presence." I had made my husband and my marriage the idol I bowed down to. It's what so many women do today, and I had fallen into that trap again and again.

I thanked Him for alerting me, after all, He is most interested in seeing us happy and restored but never at the cost of our relationship with Him. Always keeping Him first in our hearts and the one to focus on. That's what restored my marriage and that is what will complete our restoration. The more I remain transfixed on Him, the more I see my husband yearning for the things of God. Isn't that what Erin always says?

Would you recommend any of our resource in particular that helped you Tanya?

If everyone would just follow the principles in this one book *How God Can and Will Restore Your Marriage* by doing the daily lessons faithfully, your marriage can be restored. I also recommend reading the Encourager blog to keep you motivated to keep your eyes on Him.

Would you be interested in helping encourage other women Tanya?

Yes

Either way Tanya, what kind of encouragement would you like to leave women with, in conclusion?

Do not give up on your husbands and your families. God does not give up on you and me! Believe that He is faithful to make all things new and more than able to make the desert that you live, flourish with streams of water. You must fall in love with the Lord because only then will He give you the desires of your heart. But if you remain focused on your husband and your marriage, you will continue to wander in the desert. Choose Him, for yourself and for the sake of your family!

Chapter 29

Katrina

"The name of the Lord is a strong tower;
The righteous runs into it and is safe."
—Proverbs 18:10

"No Way I'm Coming Back. It's Over"

What brought you to RMI? Please use this space to briefly let our readers know what your life was like when you first found us, Katrina, so our readers understand just what a miracle your restoration is.

Katrina, how did your restoration actually begin?

In September my husband left home after another fight, it was actually me who told him to leave.

I was always contentious and it was not the first time I told him to get out of our home. This time God allowed him to leave me, completely, so that I could be reunited with my true Love. This time he said he wanted nothing to do with me. Once I calmed down I called him (with an attitude) and said, "Okay you can come back now" and he responded, "No way I'm coming back. It's over."

How did God change your situation Katrina as you sought Him wholeheartedly?

God began to show me, during this huge reality check, who I had been to my husband. He began to illuminate all my mistakes in order to mold me into a wise woman rather than a fool who tore her house down on a regular basis.

After I admitted my contentious and rebellious behavior, after I really saw the true me, I was able to work with the Lord in order to change. That's when God began to give me a daily makeover. Day after day the person He wanted me to be began to appear and the old me began to die a thousand deaths. Was it pleasant? No! It was painful and heartbreaking, but what I discovered was a Love I'd never imagined. A love I'd been looking for all of my life. A love that could keep me sane and calm and that filled the void that had made me act in such a disgusting manner.

What principles, from God's Word (or through our resources), Katrina, did the Lord teach you during this trial?

God taught me to have patience. In His Word, He always showed me the reason for my trials and tribulations, how it was meant to change me. He also gave me the strength to continue on the hardest days when I thought of giving up. My HH held my hand and sometimes carried me, but each day I kept moving ahead in my journey choosing not to take my eyes off of Him.

I always thought about the story of Jonah and knew that I was passing through the fish's mouth, but that at the right time the Lord would rescue me. He showed me it was there in the darkness that I'd have to face the way I'd always been.

He taught me to have real faith, because before I thought I had faith, until I realized that I had to believe even if all circumstances were unfavorable. During this journey, I learned to trust and give myself to the Lord completely. To want and need and live for nothing and no one else but Him.

What were the most difficult times that God helped you through Katrina?

Every time I heard about my husband and what was going on (by "friends" and family who blamed him for my brokenness), He would give me a portion of His Word that I would bathe in and cling to. I'd turn my face to Him and He comforted me. When those rumors didn't destroy me, the enemy turned up the heat. One day I saw my husband out with the OW and it was easy to see that they were having fun. The enemy bombarded my mind, reminding me of how I was suffering while he was enjoying his freedom from me.

My HH helped me on those days when nothing seemed to happen for good, when I looked at things from human eyes in the depths of despair. He said things were happening, things were changing, but they were hidden where only He could see. Then instead of running or cringing because of these episodes, I began to cherish these moments in my heart. The pain left, the love I felt for Him increased and no one but Him mattered.

God loved me to the point of sending His Son, not just to save me, but to send me a Lover of my soul. Someone who would be with me all the time and comforted me as His bride. Thank You Heavenly Father for this gift!

Katrina, what was the "turning point" of your restoration?

The turning point was when I absolutely trusted God and let my husband go. I took both hands of my HH and all I could see was Him. I began to seek the things of God, ministering to other women, encouraging them to find and experience the love of a true Husband. It was then that I saw that little by little my husband was becoming interested in me and he was always looking for me, just to talk about random things.

I began to see that all the promises of God in our lives that I'd been given during my darkest days, were now being seen by me and everyone else. This is when the enemy tried every single one of his schemes on me. Each time, I took them as a sign that good was about to happen, and began to get closer to my HH even more.

Rumors increased about my husband, but I once again trusted Him, chose to wait and chose not to care if I had a husband. I simply gave all my needs to the Lord, my true Husband, and this was when everything began to change ...

Tell us HOW it happened Katrina? Did your husband just walk in the front door? Katrina, did you suspect or could you tell you were close to being restored?

Everything started to change when my husband decided to come home to see our new baby. Right after his birth, I always took him to see his father, but this time he decided to come over and see our baby at our home. Thank You, God!!! It is You who restores, at your appointed time, which was when it was important for our son to have a father in the home.

That day we talked a lot, about nothing at all and laughed over so many silly things. It was so nice, so good, so very pleasant. When he left he asked about coming again and I mentioned that we'd be gone, having been invited to a children's party. Without planning to, I asked if he'd like to join us and he pulled back and said, he would think about it.

Of course, I realized how foolish this was, and told my HH to please use this blunder for good so it wouldn't damage what I could see my son needed now.

On Saturday, the day of the party, he sent a message saying he couldn't go and why, and I replied, "Okay, sure, thanks for letting me know" along with a smiley face. I got up to get ready when another text came in, he wanted to invite me to a barbecue at our friends' house, and he wanted me to bring our baby boy. I asked the Lord what to say, then sent a reply accepting his invitation, "Yes, that would be nice, we'd love to join you."

At the barbecue, it was me, him, our son, his parents and siblings, plus another couple of his close friends. At the end of the day, when we were about to leave, I fell into a deep pit, a crafty scheme of the enemy. I foolishly asked if I could talk to him alone, he coldly told me, no, and turned quickly to walk away.

The truth is, I really had nothing to say, but I know he took it as the way I once had been, the woman who used to sit him down to lecture him.

I was discouraged, thinking to myself, "you'll never change, you're hopeless." That night he took me home without either of us saying a word to each other. The moment I arrived home and got our son in bed, I hurried to the bathroom and said to God (because I couldn't face my HH): "Dear God, I cannot take it anymore, I do not want to deceive myself anymore that I'll ever change/ I surrender my life in Your hands, do not let me live like this anymore, please let it be me and my HH!!! I don't want a restored marriage anymore!"

When I finally felt at peace, once I was able to talk to my HH and feel His love for me, wrapping me like a warm blanket, I went back to my room to get ready. I picked up my cell phone to put it on the dresser and there was a message from my husband apologizing for not having talked to me. He said he wanted to talk and gave me a time to meet with him on the following day.

Beloved, God is so merciful and true to His Word. When we stop wanting and seeking a husband, when we want His Son, our HH, He shows us His miracles. And since I hadn't replied right back, my husband called and said he'd come over and bring lunch so we could eat at home. He said that at the barbecue he'd mentioned about him coming over to help me with my taxes and that's when he said, "I'll do your taxes, and while I'm there, we can take this time to talk. Talk about us."

For the first time, I felt him much more loving and caring than I'd ever remembered him being. I was excited but fearful that our marriage was about to be restored, however before he left he told me that he still did not feel comfortable coming home. I said that I respected him and would be more than happy to let him go. I know he was surprised, while I was relieved, to be honest.

The full effects of honestly letting go led to him inviting me to go to the movies a day later. At the movies, we kissed, and surprisingly, it was wonderful. I really thought it wasn't true that if we really were in love with our HH we could feel close to our earthly husbands.

Yet, the enemy was not about to give up. A few days later one of our mutual friends had a baby and we went to visit her. When we left the hospital we stayed in the car, like we were dating again. Then my cell phone rang and when I answered it was a woman who I could tell was angry. Then she blurted out that my husband was cheating on me! It was so loud, my husband heard what she'd said, and he got pale and unresponsive. I honestly thought he'd had a heart attack!

Beloved, do you remember when Erin says that when the restoration is near, the enemy rises up to bring us down? That was what happened, and at the time, I realized that God was protecting me when He did not allow me to know this beforehand. Then something amazing happened. At that moment I was transformed by the power of His love to the point I realized I didn't feel any anger, I felt no sorrow, and I felt absolutely NO pain. I sat there quietly in perfect peace. It was my husband who was feeling the full effects of what was happening.

After several minutes my husband told me that soon after we separated, he became involved with a person at his work and that a while ago, several weeks back before the barbecue, he began to feel ashamed of what he was doing and ended everything with her—because he wanted to come back home, GLORY TO GOD!!!!

He asked me to forgive him, he said that he was ashamed and regretted everything and that during this time of separation, he had wanted to return home several times, but he felt ashamed because he knew he'd have to confess what he'd done. He went on to say that he had never stopped loving me, that he got involved with her because of the hurt that he'd felt each time I threw him out, but that was no excuse for what he'd done.

My husband came home that day, moving in all of his things. I asked God to make him more affectionate, because I could tell he didn't feel worthy of being loved. I told God I would always submit to my HH and keep Him first in my heart. Surprisingly, that very same day my husband started to praise me saying I was such a "wise woman" and sending messages throughout the day just to say that he loved me!!!

Would you recommend any of our resource in particular that helped you Katrina?

Yes, the book *How God Can and Will Restore Your Marriage* was paramount in my restoration!!! Honestly, I have gone through all your resources and tell everyone in marriage troubles to devour everything in order to be ready for whatever the enemy throws at you.

Would you be interested in helping encourage other women Katrina?

Yes, I would.

Either way Katrina, what kind of encouragement would you like to leave women with, in conclusion?

Beloved, when we serve God and take His Son as our HH. If we follow in the footsteps of His truth during our journey, everything will work out for good. It was God who turned my husband to want to come back to our home. It was also Him who turned it away from me long enough for me to really change due only to His love and His truths.

Today He did what I even doubted could happen. Beloved, He loves us and wants to give us a makeover. He wants us to be the best we can be, and be loved by the Man of our dreams. All honor, glory, and praise be given to God the Father and His Son—the Author and Finisher of our faith!

Do not give up, do not give up, do not give up!!!! Keep moving forward along your restoration journey no matter how discouraging or painful.

The Lord is with us, let Him be your Man, I am overflowing with gratitude. Thank you, Erin. Thank You, dear HH.

Chapter 30

Guadalupe

"Their faces shall never be ashamed"
—Psalm 34:5

"The Cover Says It—How GOD Will Restore!"

Guadalupe, how did your restoration actually begin?

I had been married for almost 40 years when I began my journey. I never imagined in a million years that I'd be asked to go through so much suffering and humiliation. It happened rather suddenly when my husband began to ignore me, stay away from home and not care about anything at all he'd been interested in before.

One day I heard his cell phone ringing and when I walked by and looked at it—it had a woman's face on it. I didn't dare pick it up, besides I was so stunned I just stood there and stared. After it stopped, that's when texts started to come in, and I could read the messages that were being sent by this other woman.

It was so strange what was happening. Soon I realized that he had formed an intimate relationship with a woman from his work, and I must confess that my world fell apart. I cried a lot, nonstop, and I was without any direction to know what to do. I was ashamed, so I told no one, so for a time I suffered entirely alone. It was the shame that kept me from talking to anyone. Then one day, a day of deep desperation, I spoke to a pastor of a church I'd driven by. And I told everything to this pastor, explaining what was happening and he advised me to trust God and that this battle would be won on my knees, with my face on the ground.

Knowing I still needed to find help, I opened my laptop and began looking for help on the internet begging God to help me. That's when I found your life changing book, *How God Can and Will Restore Your Marriage*. I read the first chapter on your site and knew that GOD was speaking to me. I can't explain the kind of joy I felt, from the moment I read the title of your book. Immediately instead of not knowing what to do, my thoughts became perfectly clear, it was God telling me that He would restore my marriage.

With the Lord to help me, I began reading, marking the book and then later found your evaluation and was offered your free course. Though my life began again, my life at home, specifically my situation with my husband became worse. He was even more distant if that was possible, ignoring me entirely. Though he never told me, and I didn't ask, I knew things were getting worse.

A week or so later, I made my biggest mistake even though I knew better. I asked him what was going on, and he said nothing. Sensing this was God protecting me I said no more. But a day later I began pressing him and then that's the day he just blurted out about the OW. He said he had a deep love for this OW and he'd made promises of love to her and that meant a future with her!

Up until that day, I had been somewhat spared, but ignoring His truth hurt like nothing I'd felt before. I felt dirtied and like all our years together had meant nothing to him. I honestly thought what he was doing was something temporary and everything with this OW would soon be over, but on this day, the day I pushed him to voice what was going on, I saw in him the conviction that he was Indeed in love with this woman. He confessed to me that he could not help himself, that it was something new that he had never felt in his life. What a horrible fool I'd been.

After this fateful day, he began getting ready to leave me and looked into selling our home. He'd only spend a few minutes coming and going and all I can say is that there is no way I can describe all the suffering and humiliation I went through. He'd make a point of saying each time he was getting ready that he never loved me. That I should be honest because the only reason we'd married was that I got pregnant and because of the man he was, he did what was right. But now that the children were grown he wanted a life he chose for himself not one forced on him. He told me that at one time he wanted to be my prince, but because I'd been so far from being a princess (because I nagged and made sure I won every argument) that he'd found himself a kinder, lovelier princess to be with. That, for the first time in his life, he really experienced love and that he never knew love before he met her.

Hearing this over and over felt like every part of me had been cut to pieces. Every conversation he had after that was praises for the new princess in his life, which left me humiliated. That's when I finally learned to shut my mouth, stop talking and let God begin my transformation.

How did God change your situation Guadalupe as you sought Him wholeheartedly?

After reading the book *How God Can and Will Restore Your Marriage* so many times (I bought three that fell apart because I wore them out), I began to take a new position as His bride, His princess! It began when I recognized all my mistakes throughout our marriage and discovered what being *A Wise Woman* meant. It was not the wise cracking, mocking and the demeaning woman that I'd been in my marriage. Instead, I needed to become the quiet and gentle spirit that pleased God and my HH first.

One day I finally was forced to tell my children about our separation, but I refused to talk about their father or the OW they'd found out he was involved with.

The more I studied your books and looked up each verse, marked it in my Bible and made cards for the verses that I knew I needed to consume daily, the quicker the days went by and I began to feel stronger and stronger. The mud my husband felt he needed to throw at me each time he came over, no longer caused me as much pain. It was by God's grace and the love I had as my HH's bride that my entire demeanor began to change. I began to dedicate myself to being the wife I read about in *workers@home*, washing his clothes and even ironing—something I never did as the professed feminist I was. I learned to cook and would leave a plate for him when I knew he'd be coming.

The biggest surprise I think was when he came in to find our house tidy. That was the first time he initiated intimacy that we hadn't had for years. Afterward, he stated he felt guilty for cheating on her, that we did need to remain separated and he talked about getting a divorce. But I knew this was a good sign, it meant we were getting closer to God restoring our marriage.

I knew the delay was because God wasn't done molding me yet, making me into His perfect bride and princess, which I fully began to enjoy.

What principles, from God's Word (or through our resources), Guadalupe, did the Lord teach you during this trial?

The verse that changed my thinking was Proverbs 21:1 "The king's heart is like channels of water in the hand of the LORD; He turns it wherever He wishes" especially after my husband told me I wasn't his princess. Like Erin said she found a verse that changed everything, this verse was mine. I'd discovered this when reading the first chapter of *How God Can and Will Restore Your Marriage*, and it was just something He reminded me of often. Though my husband said he did not want our marriage, God's restoration would happen the moment He chose to turn his heart back, once I was my HH's princess and I looked fully into being His bride.

What were the most difficult times that God helped you through Guadalupe?

On the weekends it was very difficult because he would get ready to go out with the OW. Often to prepare and get in the mood he would drink excessively. While he was getting ready he ignored me and didn't talk to me, but when he came home, he'd storm into our bedroom and begin to mock me. It hurt a lot to hear all those nights when he would be so full of venom and I couldn't help feeling like the worst woman on this earth. Yet, when he was done, I would roll over and speak to my HH, who'd wrap me in His loving arms whispering His words of love to me.

Guadalupe, what was the "turning point" of your restoration?

One day when I was returning home from shopping, I clearly heard in my heart the following phrase, "The enemy is about to throw his final party and destroy you forever" and when I got home, I found my husband had gone into our home and cleared everything out. It was unbelievable but I wasn't shaken. I drove to a friend's home and calmly said that my husband had left home and would it be okay if I stay with her. Before I went to sleep that night, I opened my bible (thankful I carried it with me) and the Lord gave me the word Hebrews 11:30

"By faith the walls of Jericho fell down after they had been encircled for seven days."

For seven days I envisioned my faith surrounding my home, my marriage and my husband. On the seventh day, I got a call from my husband asking me to meet him. After all our years of marriage, I never saw my husband cry, but when we met he began to weep saying he had a change of heart and knew he'd been a fool. He begged me to take him back.

Tell us HOW it happened Guadalupe? Did your husband just walk in the front door?

After the week at my friends, he called asking if we could talk. I confess that I felt as if my heart would jump out of my chest. When we met I spoke as little as possible, and simply nodded my head as I listened.

Next week will mark the one year anniversary of when my husband came back and we moved back into our home. I am very grateful to God and find myself wanting more and more of my HH because human love can never compare to heavenly love.

I often hear my husband whispering softly, "I love you" and he has treated me as he said, his princess. He's always remained loving, caring about me and even helps me with things around the house. And due to the love I get from my HH, I am able to love my husband more than I was ever able to.

I keep my *Wise Woman* next to my bed and he has his *Wise Man* that the ministry sent him.

Yet, what I want to say is that I am so thankful God Who chose to take me into the desert so He could show me how wrong I was, and how even an older woman is able to change. Thank you, Lord, for choosing me as your bride and princess.

Now my conversations are primarily with my Husband rather than being the nagging wife to my earthly husband. And though the past may come up, I am always careful not to let anything influence what God has done because it's very easy for the enemy to return to steal from us again, so I must remain vigilant in my relationship with Him!

Would you recommend any of our resource in particular that helped you, Guadalupe?

Absolutely, the book *How God Can and Will Restore Your Marriage* and once you've come through your crisis, to switch over to *A Wise Woman* and *workers@home* to prepare for your husband returning.

Would you be interested in helping encourage other women Guadalupe?

Yes, I truly would.

Either way Guadalupe, what kind of encouragement would you like to leave women with, in conclusion?

Dear bride, never give up on what God said He would do—restore your marriage. But remember it's during our time in the desert when He will mean the most to us. You can choose to follow what Erin's books say and what the Bible says, but it's you who will decide to obey or neglect the truth. Remember that He hears us and is with us in our darkest moments when we are suffering our greatest anguish. If you find the Lord as your HH, you will find He can welcome you to a place where He will calm you, and give you utter peace. From the moment He really is your HH, you will never be alone. Remember this fight is not yours and you can't restore your marriage. The *RYM* cover says it, it's how GOD will restore. And when He is fighting for you, you will not lose the war. Just seek and find your HH, giving Him everything in your heart because He guarantees us a life of abundance, overflowing with happiness!

Chapter 31

Florencia

*"...And to God I would I commit my cause,
who does great things..."*
—Job 5:8-9

"We Have Lost Our Way"

Florencia, how did your restoration actually begin?

A friend of mine had told me about how God had restored other marriages and relationships. That's when His words reminded me how important God is in my life. He is my Father, who loved me and wanted to lead me to all prosperity. He wants to make sure all goes well with my soul. Then I later had this confirmed with audiobooks I listened to in Spanish from the author Erin Thiele that spoke everything I had been asking Him about.

How did God change your situation Florencia as you sought Him wholeheartedly?

God used the testimony of my friend who assured me that God can restore a marriage or relationship. Her witness and what He had done in her life, restoring her marriage when she listened to the audiobooks, relieved my anxiety. Later more was confirmed when God took me along my journey using the book I bought from RMI.

What principles, from God's Word (or through our resources), Florencia, did the Lord teach you during this trial?

He taught me to speak kind and loving words. Do not investigate what your husband is doing. Do not confront your husband with your suspicions but believe only in what He says or explains. Look to God, read the Bible! Stand in the gap.

What were the most difficult times that God helped you through Florencia?

Testing, a lot of testing, during which He gave me His grace at the time I needed it. He wanted to shield me from so many things He didn't want me to see or know about. In my foolishness (before knowing the principles of the book God can and will restore your marriage) one day I was trying to follow my EH in my vehicle. It was right in front of me but because God loves me, I lost sight of it before I had time to do something even more foolish.

Florencia, what was the "turning point" of your restoration?

I think my restoration was more of a process. It's difficult to pinpoint a single moment because there were so many, but I always think back to the dream that God sent me, before my journey began, long before I knew of my husband's unfaithfulness. That was the turning point for me.

Tell us HOW it happened Florencia? Did your husband just walk in the front door?

We were in communication after a time when he'd contacted me, requesting certain dates for him to visit. During these visits he said he had noticed so many amazing changes in me and in my life. Then later he started looking to me to help him with the pressures of his work. Very soon he realized he wanted me for his wife again.

Florencia, did you suspect or could you tell you were close to being restored?

Yes. During some tests while reading the section on Contentment, I found contentment but God spoke to me about restoration that He said was about to happen and I needed to find Contentment in the challenges of being restored because it was about to happen.

Would you recommend any of our resource in particular that helped you Florencia?

Number one is *How God Can and Will Restore Your Marriage*. With this alone, listening to the audiobooks and reading the book as a roadmap, any marriage can be restored as long as you have the right heart and follow the principles, not skipping any.

Do you have favorite Bible verses you would like to share with women who read your testimony? Or promises he gave you?

Daniel 10:12 "Do not be afraid, Daniel. From the very first day that you began to pursue understanding and humble yourself before your God, your words have been heard. I have been sent in response to what you've said."

Joel 2:12 MSG "But there's also this, it's not too late— God's personal Message!—"Come back to me and really mean it! Come fasting and weeping, sorry for your sins!"

Luke 7:38 "and standing behind Him at His feet, weeping, she began to wet His feet with her tears, and kept wiping them with the hair of her head, and kissing His feet and anointing them with the perfume."

Luke 7:44 "Turning toward the woman, He said to Simon, 'Do you see this woman? I entered your house; you gave Me no water for My feet, but she has wet My feet with her tears and wiped them with her hair.'"

Would you be interested in helping encourage other women Florencia?

Yes

Either way Florencia, what kind of encouragement would you like to leave women with, in conclusion?

There is a reason for this pain and brokenness you're experiencing. It's how God, our Father and Creator, calls us in order for us to return to Him. Our foolish ways bankrupt us, but for women to understand their perfect design and embrace that we need to find and follow the narrow path, we must first realize we have lost our way and cry out to Him to change us.

Chapter 32

Fernanda

"Oh give thanks to the Lord;
call upon his name; make known
his deeds among the peoples!"
—Psalm 105:1

"Took the Keys off His Keychain"

Fernanda, how did your restoration actually begin?

My five-year marriage had been marked by many trials, mostly due to my husband who grew up in an unfavorable environment and broken family. Rather than having a real family, he grew up amongst friends who stayed close all the way into adulthood. Unfortunately, these friendships were, in fact, a prison controlled by the enemy. Though most were married, the majority of their time was spent at bars, drinking beer and watching games, at least four to five times a week.

On Sundays when we went to see his family, he would drop us off and spend the whole afternoon at the bar with these same friends. There was a time when my brother-in-law advised him to pay more attention to his family because he could lose me, but he said that if I tried to interfere with his friendships, I would lose.

So, the truth is, I was always alone, but I did not complain. I just decided to keep praying and asking God to get him out of this entanglement. I fasted, I cried out to God. But it seemed like this life would be my destiny until I died.

In January, there was a week that he went to the bar every night. Then on Saturday and Sunday, he spent the whole day there. My sadness turned to bitterness, so I decided to ask him not to go, at least not for so many days each week because our two-year-old son and I missed him so much.

Instead of being sympathetic, he became aggressive, replying that nothing was good enough for me. This "talk" resulted in him not talking to me for five days and when he'd come to bed, he would lay down and make sure he turned his back on me so I knew how much he despised me. This lasted until the day I ended our marriage. I got up in the morning and left a message that our marriage was over, and that I did not deserve to live in so much loneliness and contempt. I took the keys to our house off his keychain and left only those of his mother's house. And I went to work while he still slept.

When he woke up, he noticed my note and he went crazy, calling me but I did not answer. Then he became very angry and told the whole family that he would never forgive me for having humiliated him so much.

After some time of being separated, instead of missing me, he went to the church and met a girl and began to invest in a new relationship. I almost died when I found out. Everything in my life began to spiral downward with no way out.

How did God change your situation Fernanda as you sought Him wholeheartedly?

In my desperation I began to beg God for a way out of the mess I'd created. Because of my attitude, that was entirely without wisdom, I had thrown him into someone else's arms. I began to seek prayers on the Internet to strengthen myself, and that's when God guided me to the Marriage Help site, HopeAtLast.com and I began to read the book *How God Can and Will Restore Your Marriage*. Reading that book opened my eyes and I was aghast to meet the woman I really was.

What principles, from God's Word (or through our resources), Fernanda, did the Lord teach you during this trial?

God has searched my heart and revealed to me how much I've been a contentious and overbearing woman the entire time. And I always believed I had done the best, was the best wife ever, because I thought I was putting up with so much! With every verse that I read and began pondering, God was using them, and I began appraising myself and every horrible discovery about me began to break me! I began to weep at the Lord's feet. This was the first time in my life I've truly known God for real and realized that I needed a Savior.

What were the most difficult times that God helped you through Fernanda?

As I passed through the desert, it was a journey that seemed to be endless. My EH did not look for me at all or try to contact me. And I knew I could not go and speak to him, because I was in obedience to entirely "let go," but I also read that I needed to ask for forgiveness if I were responsible for the end of my marriage.

So, one day I got up the courage and went to apologize for what I had done, for sending him away. I was received so coldly that my heart was broken. But still I said to myself, "Be at peace and quiet, because you did as unto God and you did not do it to try to get him back. Trust." I took a deep breath and began my daily struggle with all my love for God, and right after this is when I found my HH and His love. Finding my Abundant Life!

Fernanda, what was the "turning point" of your restoration?

It was during this period of my journey that I began to put my HH first in my life and heart. Due to my HH love, I was grateful all the time for everything, even if rebuked or corrected or shunned. I was thankful for every loss in my life because I would not have had my eyes opened to having a HH or Savior if God had not allowed my losses and suffering.

I prayed, I fasted, but this time, it was not with any sadness or bitterness in my heart as it had been during those first five years of my marriage. I prayed and fasted with utter joy, with gratitude, and as time went on, I knew I was learning to have patience, to work with God, and He was free to do His perfect will without my interference.

Tell us HOW it happened Fernanda? Did your husband just walk in the front door? Fernanda, did you suspect or could you tell you were close to being restored?

After three months without any contact, my husband called me very angry. He began to yell at me because I went to church in the middle of the week and left our son home with my mother. He said he would not take it, my being irresponsible anymore. That I had to have more responsibility or else he would ask for his custody in court. There! Is that what you want? What a pain you are to me, he said.

So, I remembered to say nothing, not be contentious and simply remain meek and wise and agree. So, I told him, "Yes, you're right, and I apologize." And he hung up. Two weeks went by when I was able to repent to my HH because I had ignored the lessons about letting go of my church because I didn't understand why this was important. Now I knew.

Two weeks later, he called me on a Saturday morning asking me if I wanted to take our son to a see a play for children and I said yes. So, he bought two tickets and gave us money to spend on a park nearby. Though I was surprised he wasn't coming with us (because that's how it sounded when he asked), I simply said, "Thank you very much."

The following week he sent me a text message asking me to make some Easter eggs for his nephews and I said I would. I brought them over to his mother's house and there he was, he was there alone. The whole family was traveling but I wasn't aware they were gone. When I finished unloading the eggs, he asked me to stay with our son, stay there at his parents, since he was alone. I accepted, saying no more. From exhaustion, I hadn't meant to, but I fell asleep on the couch and suddenly woke up because he'd picked me up and was carrying me to bed. He laid me on the bed and then he asked me to forgive him! ("Forgive" was never a word I've ever heard him say before to anyone.)

My husband began to cry, saying that God broke him down and made him see how important his family is to him. And that he had never given me the true honor that I deserved to have as his wife and the mother to our son. He told me that he felt bad about going to that bar all the time, basically, all his life and that he wants to present himself to God. To God who has freed him, set him free from his "friends" in order to know the truth and the true value of the life He gave him.

Needless to say, I broke down into tears of joy and gratitude to my Lord for having done a complete work in both our lives!! And even though I thank God, day and night, for restoring both of us, individually before bringing us together. My thanks will never be enough for the love He has shown me throughout my journey in finding my HH and His love.

Would you recommend any of our resource in particular that helped you Fernanda?

Beloved ones, I strongly recommend the book *How God Can and Will Restore Your Marriage* then continue and study *A Wise Woman*. The best way to pace you journey is to simply go through online courses because they are free. Then, when your heart is open (or broken) it's time to start *Finding the Abundant Life* Course.

Would you be interested in helping encourage other women Fernanda?

Yes, I would. All of us need to reach out to those who are hurting. I reach out at least once a week by going to prayer sites because it's there I found this ministry and HopeAtLast.com is where I send anyone that I see is broken.

Either way Fernanda, what kind of encouragement would you like to leave women with, in conclusion?

Beloved, no matter what your situation. No matter how horrible your life is now, you can find a happy ending. Trust God to make it happen. God is faithful **if** we are faithful to Him. His promises are true. Trust! Trust! Take this journey with Him, never look back and never go back!! And soon you too will find the abundant life I have found.

Chapter 33

Juliana

"Lord, I put my life in your hands.
I trust in you, my God, and
I will not be disappointed."
—Psalm 25:1-2

"Left My Marriage in God's Hands"

Juliana, how did your restoration actually begin?

Our relationship was no longer right since we let other things be more important than God and His things. We fought frequently and there was no longer any respect, affection, or admiration for each other. Then one day we had a very ugly fight and he took things and left home.

How did God change your situation Juliana as you sought Him wholeheartedly?

Through friends, I met a couple that works with people with marriage problems. Together they began to encourage me not to give up.

What principles, from God's Word (or through our resources), Juliana, did the Lord teach you during this trial?

The daily emails, along with your newsletters, were an additional incentive not to give up. Then, every time I thought about giving up, I remembered the excerpts from the *How God Can and Will Restore Your Marriage* book and the testimonies I had read in the courses I was taking.

What were the most difficult times that God helped you through Juliana?

The most difficult moments were knowing he was with the OW. Especially when I received messages from her or when I saw photos on social networks with him and the many OWs. However the Lord helped me by reassuring me and telling me ... if I am for you what does it matter who is against you?

Juliana, what was the "turning point" of your restoration?

The turning point was when I really turned everything over and left my marriage in God's hands. Then I no longer spent time calling, or looking, or talking about my husband, restoration, or my marriage. I only spoke about matters that were important, like our daughter. By me just being a happy mom to her, she was able to cope with everything and to deal with her life surrounded by His love.

Tell us HOW it happened Juliana? Did your husband just walk in the front door? Juliana, did you suspect or could you tell you were close to being restored?

My husband called me about buying an apartment for me and my daughter. During the conversation, I casually commented on the couple I had met and asked him to meet them, but only if he wanted to. To my surprise he accepted, but did not want to go alone and told me: YOU ARE MY WIFE and you have to go with me.

The next day, we went to see the apartment and he asked if I liked the new place and asked if I wanted to live there together. Glory to God!

Would you recommend any of our resource in particular that helped you Juliana?

Yes, the book *How God Can and Will Restore Your Marriage*, was the key point that taught me not to give up. Then going through your free courses and reading the newsletter also was very helpful.

Would you be interested in helping encourage other women Juliana?

Yes

Either way Juliana, what kind of encouragement would you like to leave women with, in conclusion?

That God is the only one who can and will restore your marriage, even if everyone says it is impossible, even your husband. Get God to fight for you, don't fight for your marriage yourself but do not give up trusting it will happen. It is only with God that you will win this battle.

Chapter 34

Gina

"Rejoice in hope,
be patient in tribulation,
be constant in prayer."
—Romans 12:12

"Embrace the Trials"

Gina, please tell us, how did your restoration actually begin?

How do I even begin to explain my RJ that has taken nearly 3 years?? It started by EH becoming distant and me trying to do everything I could do in my own strength to try and make him happy. It was during this time that my sister died from suicide, and on top of that tragedy, I was being investigated at work for an incident that could have had me fired, and my dad had legal issues. I began going to church a lot and it pushed my EH away. My EH was becoming increasingly depressed and he left me and our one-year old daughter. I already knew some of the principles from RMI so I knew not to stand in his way or chase him. I immediately sought the help of RMI. I thought he would only be gone a few days.

Gina, how did God change your situation as you sought Him wholeheartedly?

I immediately began the courses and I began to have peace that my marriage would be restored. I am so grateful for this ministry for giving me a road map not only to restoration but more importantly to a true relationship with the Lord. I always thought I was a Christian, but after experiencing all of these trials I found that I only sought the Lord when I needed help and I would try and pray for Him to change things the way I thought was best. I was such a control freak and actually thought I knew what was best for me. :)

I diligently did each of the daily courses offered through RMI and I began to pour out my heart in the forms. After completing all of the courses I began volunteering for RMI which has turned out to be such a great blessing to me.

The Lord gave me a verse "Therefore, since we have so great a cloud of witnesses surrounding us, let us also lay aside every encumbrance and the sin which so easily entangles us, and let us run with endurance the race that is set before us." Hebrews 12:1. I took this verse and ran with it...literally. I began running like I was running to Him. I trained and I even ran a marathon!! Wow only with His strength could I complete such a difficult task. I felt He was transforming me mentally, physically and spiritually. I fasted a lot and my life began to revolve more around the Lord and less around my EH. I was no longer consumed with fear like I was early on in my RJ.

I stopped looking to my EH for help and began to seek the Lord with every one of my needs. I never had to ask my EH for help financially, physically, emotionally or even to babysit. Whenever I had a need I would seek the Lord and He would provide either through my EH or others.

Gina, what principles, from God's Word (or through our resources), did the Lord teach you during this trial?

The principle that helped me the most was the principle of letting go. This was the hardest one for me. I was so fearful to let go because I feared that my EH would think I didn't care about him. This is really the most important thing not only with our EH, but with every area of our lives.

Another important principle that will forever change my life is that we are His Brides!! The Lord is our Heavenly Husband and He desires to take care of all of our needs.

Also overcoming the fear of tithing, due to being wrapped up in trying to please my husband rather than pleasing my HH.

Gina, what were the most difficult times that God helped you through?

Where do I even begin with this part? There were many difficult times over these last 3 years. Early on in RJ my EH told me to move on and take off my wedding ring. I accidentally saw his medical record where he asked his doctor for information about getting a vasectomy. (Thankfully I let it go and he never went through with it, but it caused me a great deal of fear.) I remember on Christmas Eve I came home to find he had taken down all of our family photos. He told me we would sell our home and file for divorce. I would fearfully agree and try and pray against it.

After nearly two years, my EH began staying at our home and was extremely depressed. I saw all of his belongings packed in his car. It was on our wedding anniversary (he forgot it was our anniversary) that he brought up divorce again. He confessed that there was an OW and he had been living with her. A couple days later he left and went back to live with OW. After going back, he filed for divorce. It was a very hard time for me. He began introducing the OW to our friends and would take our daughter to spend time with her. EH even asked me to help him fill out our divorce papers.

The hardest part of my RJ was letting go of our daughter going to spend time with OW. Reading and getting to know Amalia in Poland helped due to her experiences with her son, the OW and also the child her EH had with the OW.

The last 6 months of my journey were very intense with my EH coming back and forth between OW and me several times. He packed up all of his belongings from OW at least 3 times, but he never brought his stuff inside our home.

I share all of this now only because when I would devour the Restored Marriage Testimonies, I would always want to know details. To be honest, none of the incidents I went through cause me any pain. All of the pain is gone and the trials He brought me through only served to catapult me into His arms whenever I think of Him and His love.

Gina, what was the "turning point" of your restoration?

The turning point in my restoration was when I came to the point where it no longer affected me what EH was doing. It no longer mattered to me if I was ever restored and all I wanted to do was please the Lord. My HH had become everything to me, which I learned from the Abundant Life courses.

Gina, tell us HOW it happened? Did your husband just walk in the front door?

My EH called and I let our daughter answer the phone. He said, "tell mama I'm coming by." This was not unusual because he was at our home frequently, but I felt the Lord tell me that he was coming home. He came in and was very quiet and distracted and suddenly left and said he might come back later. I felt Him whisper to me "I'm going to finish it." That's when my EH text me and apologized for leaving suddenly and asked if he could spend

the night. I had the sense that he was gone packing up whatever belongings were left at OW's. I was right. He's had a trailer packed full of his stuff parked in our backyard for the last month that he never unpacked. He came home that night and has been here ever since and the relationship with OW has completely ended.

Did you suspect or could you tell you were close to being restored?

Yes and no. I was so content with my life with our HH. I remember the day before my EH came home. I was laying on my back porch saying how beautiful life is. It had nothing to do with my circumstances—only that I am so content with Him nothing else mattered. I had been feeling this way for the past few months but I was literally so in love with Him it didn't matter whether I was married, divorced, in an apartment or our home. Nothing mattered, only He mattered!

I felt restoration would be soon not because I saw any signs with my EH. He would flip flop back and forth between being super nice to me and then being distant and disconnected. I only felt it would be soon because truly it no longer mattered to me if I was restored. I lacked nothing and I enjoyed being His Bride. To be honest I was really enjoying my "alone" time and my freedom to spend all my time with Him.

Gina, would you recommend any of our resource in particular that helped you?

I recommend every single resource that RMI offers. The RRR Online Courses, *RYM* book, *Wise Woman* book, *Finding the Abundant Life* book. Really every single book is worth reading and rereading.

Do you have favorite Bible verses that you would like to pass on to women reading your Testimonies? Promises that He gave you?

"Therefore, since we have so great a cloud of witnesses surrounding us, let us also lay aside every encumbrance and the sin which so easily entangles us, and let us run with endurance the race that is set before us." Hebrews 12:1

Lay everything down and run to Him.

"For perhaps he was for this reason separated from you for a while, that you would have him back forever, no longer as a slave, but more than a slave, a beloved brother, especially to me, but how much more to you, both in the flesh and in the Lord. If then you regard me a partner, accept him as you would me. But if he has wronged you in any way or owes you anything, charge that to my account." Philippians 1:15-18

This was a promise the Lord gave me early on in RJ

"For My thoughts are not your thoughts, Nor are your ways My ways," declares the Lord. For as the heavens are higher than the earth, So are My ways higher than your ways And My thoughts than your thoughts." Isaiah 55:8-9

Would you be interested in helping encourage other women?

YES!! I love being an Encouraging Woman minister and recommend everyone take the courses and keep going until you sign up our Ministry Team.

Gina, what kind of encouragement would you like to leave women with, in conclusion?

Ladies, I know this RJ seems more than you can bear and is so painful at times. I will say that it is all temporary and soon you will look back and miss this special time in your life as long as you first find your HH and experience His love for you as His bride. This is happening because He is taking you higher. There is no way I would have the peace I have today had I not gone through some very intense trials. So, embrace the trials and let go of trying to help God in any way. I had to lay everything down and truly surrender everything to Him. He won't let us down and we can trust that He has a great plan for us!

Chapter 35

Antonia

"And your Redeemer is the Holy One of Israel,
Who is called the God of all the earth."
—Isaiah 54:5

"He Gave Me a Hug and Left"

Antonia, how did your restoration actually begin?

My husband has come home. Praise the name of the LORD, that he didn't just come back, but he came back broken before God. It's been almost a year since we were restored, but, I remember as if it were today—the image of him coming into the house, hugging me and crying, crying a lot. It was the most beautiful day of my life!!

Incredible too, is that on the same day he came home, he'd asked me to go to church and we went. We arrived early, we attended the service and then to my utter surprise and joy, at the time of the altar call, he stood up and walked down the aisle. Like a blink of an eye and there he was accepting JESUS, as His unique and sufficient Savior of his life ... IT WAS TOO MUCH FOR ME, IT WAS PERFECT!! Totally beyond what I could ever have imagined or dreamed.

My husband, of today, is another person than the man I married. My husband is kind, he is caring, he is attentive, he does things that I used to beg for (but no longer even need to ask), and today, he also prays and gives praise to GOD, for changing his life and marriage.

OUR God is perfect!!

It all started when I received an anonymous message on my cell phone, with a link that read: Your husband is with another woman in this photo. Wow, I was instantly in a fog, my heart skipped inside me, but for a moment I thought it was virus. Virus? That's right, I loved my husband so much that

I did not want to believe it was true, but since I'm very curious, I decided to open it and to my surprise, there he was with an OW. I felt my blood drain from my face, my head began to spin, my sight darken. It was just horrible.

When I got home, I told him to leave, but he said he would not, he said it was all a lie and he did not know that person. That was the beginning of "hell" in my life.

Everything, everything I suspected of my husband, I would not believe, not until I myself discovered him with my work colleague, that's when I knew he really was with an OW. Also because he started to change a lot. He began working nights always stating the same story that he had extra work. I stayed home alone, weekdays and weekends and nights. It was awful!! He also began treating me badly, cursing at me, sometimes he'd spend days without coming home, saying that he was at his friend's house. Yet, I found out that he was constantly giving gifts and buying presents for the OW, which only made me cry and cry. But at the same time he always told me that he wanted to stay with me.

It was then that we started looking for a house to rent and we found one, me with my hope, I thought that moving to the new house would be different and it was, it really was. On the day we moved to our new house, we were both anxious about the change especially me. Yet, it was there "I found" my happiness. I found RMI and my hope.

But, first, let me explain what happened. My husband came home and said he wanted to talk to my mother, I asked him if everything was okay, and he said, yes.

We went to my mother's house, and I saw when he left the room that she was in tears. I did not understand anything that was happening. I sat down and waited for someone to explain everything to me, that's when my husband came back in and began to speak: "I want to separate from you, I do not love you anymore, I am unhappy, I need my freedom, I married very young and I want to be free as a bird." My world fell apart in an instant!!

It was 3 hours of conversation between us: tears and despair. I begged. I begged him to stay, but it was no use, I discovered that he had been with OW for about a year - it was terrible to discover I had been so unaware of what was happening right under my nose.

After we finished talking he went home, got some clothes, went back to my mother's house, gave me a hug and left. That moment seemed like life no longer had any meaning for me. I clung to my mother and cried and cried, howled really. I felt such a huge amount of pain inside me that it seemed that I had a deep gushing wound. It was actually physical pain I was experiencing, I had never felt anything like it before.

How did God change your situation Antonia as you sought Him wholeheartedly?

Without a doubt it was when I found RMI! I searched for everything I could find on the internet, for me I was already going crazy, because only I believed in the restoration of my marriage, NOBODY else.

Then I found you, and I ordered the book and leaned on it for my life. I began to follow everything I read there, and God began to change my life in such a way that I could never have imagined. I poured myself into it, I took the courses, reading the same lesson over and over and over again. As I read, I'd stop and I'd humble myself at the feet of God and from there, He was molding me, changing me, transforming me into a new woman.

I've always been a contentious woman, fighting for everything and that's where He healed me first. I've been changing and changing and changing all due to His Word. So much so, that the people around me would say they could see something different in me. I told them it was the love of God that had invaded me.

What principles, from God's Word (or through our resources), Antonia, did the Lord teach you during this trial?

I think I became a lover of reading in this process of finding RMI. I read some other books that have helped me but for me it's the WONDERFUL book *How God Can and Will Restore Your Marriage*, that was crucial. If someone needs hope and a map to know how to change everything about themselves, this is the one to read.

What were the most difficult times that God helped you through Antonia?

The most difficult times were when people in my husband's family came to tell me what he did or did not do with OW. It was horrible and I always felt bad when I heard such things while still trying to remain gracious with a gentle and quiet spirit.

Antonia, what was the "turning point" of your restoration?

Look, to tell you the truth, I'm not sure when the turning point was, because from the beginning I always followed the concept of "letting go", never, NEVER chasing after my husband, because when he left, he said that if I called, he would not answer, if my mother called, he would not answer, if anyone in the family called, except my cousin to whom he was closest, he would not answer.

You know, from the day he left, I started to write a diary, write everything that happened to me throughout the day and evening. I wrote down everything I read and found on the internet. I wanted to look back to see how far I've come.

There were many fasts I took while I was in this desert, because I learned when fasting it's so important because of how much it strengthens us. While fasting, I spent time and I sought the Lord more, sometimes I kept wondering how I could spend so much time away from His presence. Unfortunately I had to learn to seek Him out of pain. Each day that passed, I became more attached to the Lord!!!

Tell us HOW it happened Antonia? Did your husband just walk in the front door? Antonia, did you suspect or could you tell you were close to being restored?

I think as of this day, his heart began to soften, but after that, nothing, no news, nothing. I continued in my position of expectation, of waiting on GOD.

It happened one morning while I was tidying up the house, he sent me a text message that said: "Wait on the LORD and trust that all will give Right for both of us. Thank you for being such a wonderful person. Kisses and I believe that this year, my life will take a turn for the better!"

Do you believe that?? Look, when my husband left the house, he was unmoved, he said that he had not loved me in a long time, that he did not want me in bed anymore, that he could not even kiss me, and after all this time, he send a message like that!!! Only God!!

On New Year's morning, I opened my email, and I saw an email from him with the subject: "Happy New Year." I opened the email with my heart almost jumping out of my chest and I read this: "I have been wrong, in my life, but I know that God will change it. I believe that this year we will be happy again and maybe one day forget everything that's happened ... I've been thinking a lot about you! Kisses and stay with God."

Wow, can you believe how wonderful GOD is??? From this day on, he started to get in touch with me, to send me emails, text messages, though he NEVER called me, we just were exchanging messages. During this time God was drawing me ever closer to Him. Whenever he had any news about a delivery at the apartment he was in, he would let me know. These were surprising days, but there were days when I thought I would give up, circumstances would appear, I would feel weak, I would cry, but GOD was always there to console me. There were days when I would come home, sit on my bed and call Jesus to sit by my side and talk to me, it was incredible to have a HH so close!

Would you recommend any of our resource in particular that helped you Antonia?

I certainly would begin by just recommending the RMI web site, where they'll find the life changing books. I still find how amazing it is that Erin talks about our attitudes and how we can change, just obeying GOD above all things.

Would you be interested in helping encourage other women Antonia?

Yes for sure. You know, I asked a lot from GOD, asking Him to show me women who were going through the same situation as me, and to my joy, the LORD entrusted me and every day HE has put hurting women in my path, so that I can comfort them and pray and send them to your site.

Either way Antonia, what kind of encouragement would you like to leave women with, in conclusion?

As I said earlier, seeking GOD above all things and obeying Him— that is all He wants from us and that's what shows Him that we love Him. We need to love Him more than anyone, including our earthly husband.

This is what happened to me, I loved my earthly husband so much, I loved him so much, that the Lord had to remove him from my life, so that I could love my Heavenly Husband more than anyone or anything in this world, and this was the best thing that happened. This has meant more than my restoration.

"Today, I love my husband even more than before, but it's different, because I love my Lord, my HH above him and anyone else!!

Chapter 36

Margaret

"But the Lord stood with me,
and strengthened me."
—2 Timothy 4:17

"He Was My Everything"

How did your restoration actually begin Margaret?

My restoration began when I realized that our God is a God of love and that He didn't throw me in the furnace to burn, but to draw me closer to Him. I accepted that God was working in me and who I am in Him. It wasn't about my EH or his sins because he doesn't know the Lord "yet." It was about me and how God was preparing me to depend on Him.

My beloved sisters, God restored my marriage with a not yet believer husband (he will be a Godly man, I prophesied in the name of Jesus!)

Yes, he had another woman! Yes, he moved out! Yes, he bought all the furniture for his new apartment! Yes, he said that he didn't love me anymore, and I have been through everything you are going through right now!!

Throughout my restoration journey, I constantly questioned if my marriage was going to be restored for several reasons: I was born again when I was 16 years old and I knew that I shouldn't have married an unbeliever. I had never really let God have His will in my emotional life. It's embarrassing to share this, but I used to think to myself: God can't have anyone better for me than this man! I have to marry him.

I pressured my husband to get married because we were moving countries and I didn't want to move overseas only as his fiancé. I never asked God if this was His will at the time. I used to question myself when the crises started, was it really God who joined us together? "What therefore God has joined together, let not man separate." Was it really God or MYSELF who joined us together?

It was difficult for me to believe that God wanted to restore my marriage because I have been very disobedient to His word. But sisters, our HH is forgiving and merciful!

I was a jealous, unsubmissive wife. I didn't honour my husband and I thought that I was better than him. I was full of myself. I started to feel rejected, unloved, and the wall between my husband and I started to get bigger and bigger. We lived in the same house in this situation for over a year and he decided to move from home 9 months ago. Soon after, I found out that he was going on a holiday with the OW. My world fell apart and I ran to the only One who could comfort me, our Beloved.

Margaret, how did God change your situation as you sought Him wholeheartedly?

God changed me and how I was seeing everything around me. He showed me through His Word how He would like me to be and to behave. The closer I got to Him, the more He changed me. My HH broke me with so much love! He kindly showed me through pain that I was the one who was an adulteress in the first place when I was putting my will first, not God's will.

He showed me that I was a pride Pharisee, full of myself. He transformed me into a humble Godly woman, with a quiet spirit and mainly, completely submitted to His Word and will.

The situation around me didn't seem to change, but how I was seeing things, that was constantly changing. I fixed my eyes on the Lord and **He was my Everything**: My Husband, my Strength, my Comfort, my Friend, my Guide and my only Fountain of Happiness.

All I wanted was to spend my life with my HH.

What principles, from God's Word (or through our resources), did the Lord teach you during this trial Margaret?

How God Can and Will Restore Your Marriage was the best resource I found in my trial. It fed me and it really changed me. I read every line of it, realizing it as the single truth of God and it is fact! I practiced every teaching in the book and ladies, they work! I was washed and cleansed by the Word of God! Everything we need is in the Bible. If we follow closely what God command us to do, we will be successful in everything we do.

The principles that I have applied were:

See my sins only

The work is in me, not on other people

Let God be God in my life: my First Love, being the first in my life

Don't go on FaceBook or try to know anything related to the OW

Be quiet

Have a quiet spirit

Don't bring problems to your husband

Agree with my adversary

Wait in the Lord because He is perfect and His timing is perfect

Don't go after my husband: don't ask him what he is doing, who he is with....

Be kind and happy when he is around

Don't take the wedding ring off

Keep the house and his stuff exactly how he left it

Margaret, what were the most difficult times that God helped you through?

Being quiet! Keeping my mouth closed! People would come to me to say what he was doing and actually my 3-year-old son started to say the OW name and her children's name and God gave me the grace to keep quiet, not mentioning anything to my EH.

The OW's husband contacted me as well and God gave me strength to delete the conversation and not to reply to him.

God sustained me during this whole 9 months separated. Every single second of it was painful and very difficult.

Margaret, what was the "turning point" of your restoration?

The turning point of my restoration was when I had my EH (we were separated for 9 months) and his family over for Christmas. God moved and we spent Christmas as a family, and this moved my husband's heart and gave me the chance to show him all the amazing work that my HH was doing in me during the 9 months that we were separated. My husband asked me if I still had some of his clothes in the house on Christmas day. I told him that it was in his chest of drawers just like he left it. Oh sisters, how I prophesied upon that chest of drawers that all his clothes were going to be back again and they are now!

They stayed over for 3 days (all not yet believers) and as soon as they left, I anointed the house and cried on my HH's feet because I missed Him so much! During these 3 days, I didn't hear my worship songs, didn't hear my favourite preachers and didn't pour out my heart with tears before my HH like I normally do. I just missed Him so much!

When my husband and his family left the house, I ran to my HH's feet praising Him because I missed His presence for the last 2 days that I had people over! I longed for my HH more than words could describe! This was the turning point of my restoration as everyone else says!

I realized I loved my new life with my 3-year-old son and my HH. I no longer watched TV or listened to any world music, and having the TV on for these 3 days and world music in my house really upset me. I didn't want to live this life anymore. I genuinely opened my heart to the Lord and told Him that I was happy with my new life with Him and that I didn't want my husband back if he wasn't transformed by Him. When I really accepted the Lord as my Husband, He changed my situation.

Margaret, tell us HOW it happened? Did your husband just walk in the front door?

It really happened out of nowhere! My EH was being very rude with me right before Christmas and he changed in the week between Christmas and New Year's. I went to the church on the 29th of December and my friend had a vision while she was praying for me that my husband was blind but he desperately wanted to see! I got back home on that day and all I could do was cry out for the blood of Jesus to set my EH free from the spiritual blindness. All of the sudden he started to change! He started to share more photos of my son, checking how my day was going and even asked for me to pray for him. I knew that something was happening. I believed in that vision that the Lord gave to my friend. On the night of December 31st to January 1st, I had a dream that my EH had his wedding ring back on. He looked at it and he said: "I want a new one!"

Yes sisters, on that same morning my EH came to pick up my son with his wedding ring back on! Just like that! I couldn't be more surprised. He invited me to go to the park with him and my son and I gladly said yes! He didn't mention anything until we were back at home. I offered him a cup of tea and kindly said: "I am glad to see your wedding ring back on!" He smiled and he said: "New Year, new life!"

To the GLORY of the Lord!!! In fractions of seconds, he started to answer everything that I was praying for two years: He said that he loved even more now, that he never felt like he was at home in his rented flat, that he missed me, how much more he appreciated me. That he was truly sorry for everything he had done, and how much he admired me and that he was miserable during all the time we were separated and that he prayed! He said that he would cry almost every day. And in the end, he asked if he could move back in even having his rental contract for more 4 months!

Oh how I have prayed to hear all these things! God answered to all my prayers in seconds!

Margaret did you suspect or could you tell you were close to being restored?

Not until 3 days before he moved back. I started to see something changing after my friend's vision, but I couldn't tell that he was coming back home.

Would you recommend any of our resource in particular that helped you?

Do all the RRR Online Courses in the RMI website! Ready all the testimonials because this will give you strength and faith. If God restored my marriage, He will restore yours as well! *How God Can and Will Restore Your Marriage* you must read and apply all the principles and let the Lord change you for His glory.

How God Can and Will Restore Your Marriage was real spiritual food to me and I was transformed by the Word of God, even after 15 years going to the church! I can't put in words the strength and hope that the RYM book and all your testimonials gave me. I followed every single principle of the book and the scriptures, and I have experienced great miracles!

Margaret, do you have favorite Bible verses that you would like to pass on to women reading your Testimonies? Promises that He gave you?

I have so many! :)

Would you be interested in helping encourage other women?

Yes!!

Margaret, what kind of encouragement would you like to leave women with, in conclusion?

Our HH is wonderful! I don't have words to describe Him! If God restored my marriage He will restore yours!

I did everything wrong and my HH still had mercy on me! I was a believer (not converted properly). I got married to an unbeliever, had a my son before getting married.... I questioned the Lord if actually my marriage was out of His will...Yes, your marriage is God's will and He will restore it! Just believe!

Chapter 37

Pilar

"It is the Lord who goes before you.
He will be with you; he will not leave
you or forsake you. Do not fear or be dismayed."
—Deuteronomy 31:8

"Always Here For Us!"

Pilar, how did your restoration actually begin?

My restoration journey began a year ago in April, when my EH, over the phone, told me we needed to take some time apart from each other. He told me he needed his freedom and was tired of all the fighting and all the arguments. I was shocked especially since this had happened 2 years before but back then I didn't know about RMI, so I didn't know what to do (but thanks to my Beloved) I know now.

My HH did restore my marriage to my EH once before, but once again I was that foolish, contentious women who tore her house down with her own hands, and once again there was another OW.

As the days went by, after the conversation we had over the phone, I began asking questions, demanding answers, screaming, snooping on Facebook, telling EH he was going to regret everything and it would probably be too late, and even though I never told my family about what was going on. Back then, I did get my in-laws involved (we all live in the same house) since we had gotten really close and they weren't always ok with the things he did. I also let my sister-in laws know what was happening and right away they took my side. Even though I am very grateful with them for always being there for me, I now know I did everything wrong and I have repented for it because I put my EH's own family against him.

I would try to put a strong face in front of everyone, but inside I was broken. God was using the most important thing for me to catch my attention, the thing I would even brag about loving more than anything in this world, which was my family. My heart was with my family before being with my Beloved, but sure enough My Love got all my attention:)

How did God change your situation Pilar as you sought Him wholeheartedly?

I began to search, asking God for answers. I was very confused and hurt. One day as I was searching the web for prayers, I typed in the word restoration (can't remember and I'm not even sure why). There were several testimonies of women whose marriages got restored all thanks to the love and grace of God. I kept searching and then I came to the RMI website, which right away caught my attention and that's when God began His work in me. He opened up my blind eyes to the truth and I began to see that all these years I was the one who had been wrong. It was hard not to see what my EH was doing, but now I was seeing the faults that were in ME and I no longer wanted to point the finger at him.

What principles, from God's Word (or through our resources), Pilar, did the Lord teach you during this trial?

I began to keep my mouth shut just like my HH was teaching me to do. Believe me it was (and still is) very difficult but not impossible, Matthew 19:26, "Jesus looked at them and said, 'With man this is impossible, but with God all things are possible.'"

I also began to agree and be submissive to my EH and that was not easier either. We had different conversations about what was going on in our marriage and the first few were very difficult because I would hear from my EH how he had fallen in love with the OW and no longer had any feelings towards me. But praise the Lord, once I began to agree with him, and tell him that I loved him and just wanted *him* to be happy and I respected his decisions—he went from telling me he no longer loved me, to him feeling confused and then not being happy ever since he left the house. I could see the hate wall come down right away. At times he even told me he only felt comfortable and happy being home with us (me and our daughters) but he just couldn't come back home and wasn't fully sure why. But I did know why, it was because my Beloved knew it wasn't time. For his time is perfect.

What were the most difficult times that God helped you through Pilar?

The most difficult was when I found out about the OW. I felt like my whole life was falling apart and the enemy with his schemes and lies made me believe that my EH was moving on from me and our three daughters, and that his heart now belonged to her. What I realized after I got farther along in my journey, was that what my EH was doing to me, was what I had done to my lovely HH it hurt me to realize how unfaithful I had been to Him! I cried and repented for it and I know in my heart that my HH forgave me without a doubt.

Then my EH began spending more time with the OW and her kids than with his own. I couldn't believe he was wasting money on them and riding them in the cars that (back then I used to think) were "MY DAUGHTERS, MINE." It was hard to let go of all of that, but thanks to my Lord I started to and that's when things changed.

Pilar, what was the "turning point" of your restoration?

Through my RJ (only the Lord knows why and I know that's where HE wanted me) I was able to see, hear, and witness a lot of the things, text messages, happy moments, arguments, just the whole relationship with my EH and the OW.

I began to pray, asking my HH to help me just let go of my EH and our marriage, that now I knew in my heart I only wanted HIM and didn't want anything to bother or hurt me anymore. I would talk to Him about how sometimes I felt more comfortable with my EH being away than at home, things just felt awkward when we were together.

Tell us HOW it happened Pilar? Did your husband just walk in the front door?

My EH did go live with his sister, but never completely left. He kept going back and forth from his sister's to being back home with us. He would also go back and forth from telling me to move on and find someone better than him who deserved me, to telling me I wasn't allowed to be with anybody else and not to even think about talking or texting with anybody, meaning another guy.

Like I mentioned before, I was able to see and witness a lot of what happened in my EH's relationship with the OW, and with that I was able to see how sour their relationship began to turn. "Bitter as wormwood." They would have fights more and more. My EH began to stay home more, even though he would say in many different occasions that he would not be coming home anymore (me just leaving it in my Love's hands) he would always return for one reason or another. My EH's arguments with the OW would only get worse and worse until one day she just came, and she went, just like that, completely gone and my EH completely returned home. All glory, honor, and praise to God the Father and His Son, my HH.

My marriage has been restored and there's still a lot more about my journey, but it would take a long time to write everything down. But what I can tell you is that our HH husband loves us and He is, has and always will be here for us! Ladies we must believe, have faith and trust in our Lord and Savior and Husband, who gave His life for us to live abundantly.

Pilar, did you suspect or could you tell you were close to being restored?

I already had my HH's promise that HE would restore my marriage and I believed in His promise, so I knew it would happen. But I honestly thought it would take longer and didn't feel completely prepared. I felt and feel that there is still a lot more work to be done not only in my family but in me, especially me! But I trust that God will finish the work He began in me and my family.

Things have not been easy since EH returned home as our lessons tell us over and over. It's a new season in my restoration. I am faced with new difficult trials— but I know my Love is with me and He will not leave me nor forsake me. And now I tell my HH all the time "HE is all that I want, all that I need, and if I have Him, I will have everything that I need."

Would you recommend any of our resource in particular that helped you Pilar?

I would recommend the *How God Can and Will Restore Your Marriage* book and *A Wise Woman* book. I would also recommend the free RRR online courses, even though I confess I've struggled with finishing the courses, but will continue *Finding the Abundant Life*, because it has been such an incredibly big help —so definitely I recommend them all.

Do you have favorite Bible verses Pilar that you would like to pass on to women reading your Testimonies? Promises that He gave you?

Jesus looked at them and said, "With man this is impossible, but not with God; all things are possible with God." Mark 10:27

Whoever tries to keep their life will lose it, and whoever loses their life will preserve it. Luke 17:33

Be strong and courageous. Do not be afraid or terrified because of them, for the Lord your God goes with you; he will never leave you nor forsake you." Deuteronomy 31:6

[A Time for Everything] There is a time for everything, and a season for every activity under the heavens: a time to be born and a time to die, a time to plant and a time to uproot, a time to kill and a time to heal, a time to tear down and a time to build, ... Ecclesiastes 3:1-3

Wives, submit yourselves to your own husbands as you do to the Lord. Ephesians 5:22

Would you be interested in helping encourage other women Pilar?

I am absolutely interested in helping other women!!

Either way Pilar, what kind of encouragement would you like to leave women with, in conclusion?

My marriage has been restored and there's still a lot more to come in my journey, but it would take a long time to write everything down. But what I can tell you is that our HH, our Husband loves us and HE is, has and always will be here for us. Ladies we must believe, have faith and trust in our Lord and savior, who gave his life for us and experience His love while we journey.

Chapter 38

Isidora

"...Set your minds on things above"
—Colossians 3:2

"Get Up— I'm On My Way Home"

How did your restoration actually begin Isidora?

Wow, where to begin. Well, it began when I stopped letting everyone tickle my ears with what I wanted to hear. I started searching on the internet for marriage restoration. It was the Lord pushing me, but at that moment I described it as a force (I know better now). I have to admit I first came upon another ministry (Standers) but the way they proceed didn't agree with the little I already knew. My question was always why if God is working for us do I need to pursue my husband? If God is working for us, why do we have to put our hands in the situation? Why must we chase our EH? But then through someone I made friends with on the internet she introduced me to *How God Can and Will Restore Your Marriage* and then I found the link to RMI. I answered the questionnaire and joined the course. I took the RRR online courses got up to *A Wise Woman* and then was led by my HH to refresh my mind with the courses again.

Isidora, how did God change your situation as you sought Him wholeheartedly?

It was when I could only see my sin and realized I had put my EH on a pedestal and had put the Lord in second place. That's when things started shifting in the right direction when I acknowledged the truth. Also when I stopped defending myself and let my HH defend me asking for His will to be done. Also an important principle when I started telling Him ..."Lord You're all I want, all I need, You're Who I live for— without You, I am nothing" that I learned in FAL. At first it feels like you're just saying it, but soon it was wholeheartedly and still is! Amen!

What principles, from God's Word (or through our resources), did the Lord teach you during this trial Isidora?

SG in everything is first, also don't lean on your own understanding, agree with your adversary quickly, don't trust what you see, the biggest battle is in our minds, keep your eyes on the Lord not your circumstances are the most important I tell everyone. Over all, fill yourself with Scripture, let His Word be treasured in your heart not just head knowledge. Be still and let God be God— don't put your hand on anything, let Him do it. Learn how to be silent and listen to the Lord, don't just pray and talk to Him, you also need to listen.

Isidora, what were the most difficult times that God helped you through?

At the beginning when I hit rock bottom and started SG for myself and He started revealing His truths through His word. That's when I was accused of being demonized, crazy, a rebel, etc. And the next difficulty was when I truly let go of my EH.

Isidora what was the "turning point" of your restoration?

I had a truly huge battle within me. My HH started telling me it was time to restore my marriage and I kept trying to convince Him I wasn't ready. I told Him how we would lose our solitude our time together. I even went as far as to question Him if my EH was worth it. Big huge mistake...the storm became really fierce and I was caught in a whirlwind. I repented asked forgiveness and was reminded this was for His Glory and that this wasn't about me or us, but Him. I started falling on my face and asking for **His will to be done** and for forgiveness. The storm ragged on, believe me, but still I was filled with peace...His peace! Amen! This is the way most women finally get their restoration, what Erin says is how she felt.

Isidora, tell us HOW it happened? Did your husband just walk in the front door?

It was very late and I had been woken by my sis who had just had a small car accident and was feeling down because her husband was upset and would not talk to her (he had just bought her the car two months prior). I was dozing off but writing to her at the same time and telling her to relax, that her EH would come around and the Lord was in control and that I would be praying for her. Also I wrote to her, "I am falling asleep, love you, I will call you tomorrow"...as I was getting ready to hit the send button, I was startled when my cell began ringing. I was half asleep, so I turned on the light and couldn't believe the name on my ID caller. I gazed at it for a couple of seconds and then I answered. My EH asked what I was doing, I answered "trying to sleep" ...he laughed said "Well, don't get up out of bed, I am on my way home, I'll be there in about 30 minutes." I was surprised and said, "You know, it's kind of late for a visit" then he laughed again and said, "It's not a visit, I have all my stuff with me, I am moving back home."

Isidora did you suspect or could you tell you were close to being restored?

Sort of. I knew it was close because for weeks, if not months, I was being stretched to the point of feeling like I was breaking with more and more trials, one after another. In fact, all my utilities were about to be shut off, my car had broken the power steering, my brakes were not working correctly, and my pantry was almost bare. Along with these, there were other situations with family and extended family, like health, financial issues, and with some of their relationships hitting dark clouds like mine was in ....and I was right in the middle of everything. Everything RYM says means you're close.

Would you recommend any of our resource in particular that helped you?

All the resources helped a lot, *How God Can and Will Restore Your Marriage* is number 1, of course the Bible, *Facing Divorce Again, Finding the Abundant Life*, the Praise Reports, "Psalms" and "Proverbs", *A Wise Woman* so you're ready for staying restored, reading the Encourager every morning. I know I left some out, but they all helped in my Restoration. I recommend them all! They are a blessing and a guide in this RJ.

Isidora, do you have favorite Bible verses that you would like to pass on to women reading your Testimonies? Promises that He gave you?

"Now faith is the assurance of things hoped for, the conviction of things NOT seen." —Hebrews 11:1

"Therefore the LORD longs to be gracious to you, And therefore He waits on high to have compassion on you. For the LORD is a God of justice; How blessed are all those who long for Him." —Isaiah 30:18

"O LORD, You surround [me] with favor as with a shield." —Psalm 5:12

"For I am confident of this very thing, that He who began a good work in you will perfect it until the day of Christ Jesus"—Phil. 1:6

"Trust in the Lord with all thine heart; and lean not unto thine own understanding. In all thy ways acknowledge Him, and He shall direct thy paths"—Prov. 3:5–6 KJV

Would you be interested in helping encourage other women?

Yes I would be interested in helping other women!

Isidora, what kind of encouragement would you like to leave women with, in conclusion?

Ladies, be sure to SG in everything even in the smallest things. Fill yourselves with the Word not just head knowledge, but to hide in your heart. His Word going to lift you when you're down. Don't stop running after the Lord, pursue Him, not your EH. I can't lie, as Erin and everyone kept telling me, it was easier when my EH was not here than it is now. It's much more difficult to make time for my HH, it's not like when I was alone with just me and Him.

Don't let your guard down, you will be stretched but just try to keep your eyes on Him and know it's God who will restore you. Have faith and keep your HH first. Keep praying for us who are restored, because I will be praying for you all. Blessings for all. Amen!!!! Hallelujah!!

Chapter 39

Nicki

"And from his fullness we have
all received, grace upon grace."
—John 1:16

"Turned the Other Cheek"

Nicki, how did your restoration actually begin?

When my husband left this past January, I searched for Christian prayer sites. A fellow Christian saw my request and sent me an email. He suggested your ministry. He also told me about your book, *How God Can and Will Restore Your Marriage*. Praise God!

How did God change your situation Nicki as you sought Him wholeheartedly?

Once I received your RYM book, I began to look at my situation in a completely different way. Yes, I still cried, but I cried TO THE LORD instead of crying for my husband. Your book taught me a lot about myself and how I had to change! Praise God for opening my eyes to His Word! I found my HH soon after reading *Finding the Abundant Life* and that's when I was finally able to let go. It was very hard because I'd been in so many groups and having friends who pursued their husbands relentlessly, so I had to let go of all this first. It was easier than I thought because I was worn out. I realized this because the hate wall kept getting stronger the more I pursued my EH.

What principles, from God's Word (or through our resources), Nicki, did the Lord teach you during this trial?

Without the Lord leading me, I could never have gotten through each day feeling stronger in my spirit and due to the Love I got from my Heavenly Love. I finally let God take full control of my life and my marriage restoration. Whenever I felt the urge to call my husband, because I'd been told countless times to pursue, I instead prayed. Even after I made the mistake and sent him a card for Valentine's Day, but the struggle got easier the more I read the Word and talked to my HH asking Him to forgive me for being unfaithful to Him. I was now His and my heart needed to be fully HIS too.

Initially I was SO broken and distraught over the trials in my marriage, which led me to this ministry, but over the last couple years, I've noticed that even though for a short time I'd gone back to church and gotten involved in different things, the teachings from the beginning of RMI had stuck with me. All the biblical principles were providing a solid structure in which I could forge ahead into my restoration journey, while also encouraging and lifting others as other women have done for me. I believe that if we don't help other women, God can't help us as much as we want no matter how much we beg Him too. He will give us in the same measure as we give just as it says in Luke 6:38 and this is what I tell everyone.

What were the most difficult times that God helped you through Nicki?

One day when we spoke and I made the mistake of telling my EH I was praying for him (because I'd been part of a standers group), his response was, "Not even your prayers are going to bring me back." At that point I was at my lowest, but I soon was able to pick up and read His Word, I prayed and repented until I could feel His love again, and instead of crying for my EH, I began to cry to know the Lord as my HH. I knew He answered me and was right next to me the moment I repented of my unfaithfulness to Him, when I felt a warm sense of peace come over all of me. The Lord was telling me I would be okay. I was loved. I knew I could not fight this fight that it was His as my HH and that He is who I wanted more than anything.

Because my husband and I have both experienced infidelity in the marriage, this sin was on both sides of our marriage, it was the cause of the tremendous rift, due to the brokenness and betrayal that had plagued our union. Now that we're restored it has brought all the praises and GLORY to the most high, my HH.

Originally my EH was firm about wanting a divorce and was too hurt to carry on in our marriage, but as the RYM says, when it's time, He, God, will turn the heart back but only when we are first faithful to our HH.

Also, I had to forgive my husband. Hard? Yes, but not when you surrender your heart to your HH. God made it easier for me (and you) to have a forgiving heart once we have His heart. I learned that only He could control my anger because it's unforgiveness. And that by having my focus on my HH, my new heart would be what would win my husband back to Him and back to me.

Nicki, what was the "turning point" of your restoration?

Finding your books. First your RYM book gave me reason to believe our marriage would be restored when the Lord was ready to do His work. He taught me through this book that even though my husband was giving up, I had to trust Him with my entire being. He taught me that I, too, was at fault because I was not perfect. And the second was finding my HH so I could fully let go.

Tell us HOW it happened Nicki? Did your husband just walk in the front door?

I had to let my HH take control and lead me. After two months separated, and content with just having Him alone, I was reading my Bible. It was early and I thought it strange for the phone to ring. I heard Him say to give Him control, when I picked it up to say hello—it was my husband! He asked if we could get together to talk. He told me he had not slept all night; a voice kept telling him he needed to call me.

Praise my Lord Jesus, His Word is the Truth! He will never forsake His children. God worked in me and then worked in my husband. I give all the glory to the Lord! Although our separation only lasted about three and a half months, it felt like an eternity.

We had been married four years, but I had been with my husband for the past thirteen years. When he looked at me and said he didn't love me anymore, I was devastated. He told me our marriage was over and, no matter how much I begged, he wasn't coming back.

Nicki, did you suspect or could you tell you were close to being restored?

God is awesome if you just let Him restore you! My EH asked to meet him at church and it was there, in the pew, that we spent a few hours talking. I felt as if all my troubles were over and this was the end of this part of my Restoration Journey. My husband then said he wanted to take time talking more before coming home too quickly. Of course, I agreed, trusting the Lord to finish His work and to prepare me for what I knew would be harder...my EH home so I'd have less time with my HH.

Well, thankfully I did have more time with my HH because the enemy of course wasn't going to give up so easily after God turned my EH's heart back to me. Through "friends" I found out that my husband was with the OW on two occasions. Once again, I felt like I was being slapped in the face but that's when He reminded me He asked me to turn the other cheek, walk the extra mile and bless instead.

Later I found out it was the OW who sabotaged my EH and that's how the rumor started that they were still together. But He worked that out for good too, because when I didn't care (though it really hurt at first), my EH made sure to explain and that it made him loathe the OW.

Would you recommend any of our resource in particular that helped you Nicki?

I recommend to everyone married to read A Wise Woman and if they are in crisis RYM. A WW is important because it taught me how to be a good wife when my EH returned. I think that's why so many don't stay restored.

Erin's book *How God Can and Will Restore Your Marriage* was the best money I ever spent ever. I learned that my faith in the Lord was not what I thought it was. I had believed all my life, but I never really gave God full control of my life until I read your book. Praise God for leading me to your ministry where I found the love my life was missing!

Do you have favorite Bible verses Nicki that you would like to pass on to women reading your Testimonies? Promises that He gave you?

"But I say to you, do not resist an evil person; but whoever slaps you on your right cheek, turn the other to him also. If anyone wants to sue you and take your shirt, let him have your coat also. Whoever forces you to go one mile, go with him two. Give to him who asks of you, and do not turn away from him who wants to borrow from you." Matthew 5:39-42

"But I say unto you, That ye resist not evil: but whosoever shall smite thee on thy right cheek, turn to him the other also." Matthew 5:39 KJV

"Fear not, for you will not be put to shame; and do not feel humiliated, for you will not be disgraced; but you will forget the shame of your youth, and the reproach of your widowhood you will remember no more. For your Husband is your Maker, Whose name is the Lord of hosts; And your Redeemer is the Holy One of Israel, Who is called the God of all the earth. 'For the Lord has called you, Like a wife forsaken and grieved in spirit, Even like a wife of one's youth when she is rejected,' Says your God." Isaiah 54:4-6

"Give, and it will be given to you. They will pour into your lap a good measure—pressed down, shaken together, and running over. For by your standard of measure it will be measured to you in return." Luke 6:38

Would you be interested in helping encourage other women Nicki?

Yes. This is what He is calling me to do. After I read the RYM book about eight times, long before my marriage was restored, a friend I met in a prayer room had her sister email me as she also was going through a separation. I knew the Lord was asking me to give her encouragement. I asked for her address and sent her my book.

The only resource I had was that Restore book, but once I gave mine away, I found out about the FAL book.

Either way Nicki, what kind of encouragement would you like to leave women with, in conclusion?

Dear bride, your restoration like mine will be hard, but if you find your HH, I promise it will get easier. Yes, the enemy will try many times to wound you and discourage you, but if you just follow the principles, with Him at your side, you will make it.

I had to come to the point of being able to say, that I wrote in my journal, "At this point in my restoration journey the Lord is who I want and need. But I am open and willing should the Lord want to restore my marriage for His testimony." If you continue to worship your EH and your marriage, you'll stay pursuing the love that is fleeting and unfulfilling.

It's been over six months since my husband and I were restored, renewing our vows and I was able to fit into my same wedding dress. Now, it's together that we are able to thank God for loving us enough to save us from the enemy that has taken so many marriages. Thank you, Erin, for your wonderful ministry, for your dedication to helping women like us, and for your encouragement to continue when I wanted to give up! God bless you!!!

Lord, my HH, I give You all the praise and glory and my love! I did nothing except believe and trust in You and YOU alone.

~ Nicki in Mississippi

Chapter 40

Veronica

"And from his fullness we have all received,
grace upon grace."
—John 1:16

"Restored In Grace"

Dear ERIN:

The Lord says in his word, that if we take the precious from the vile we shall be like his mouth .... Jeremiah 15:19

And throughout all these years, you have dedicated your life precisely to understand and take the precious in you. AND IT IS JESUS ... SAME who speaks through you my Beloved ERIN, giving encouragement to ALL of us!!

I want to share with you that your Ministry was like a Powerful guide for me to find the complete restoration of my life.

Being RESTORED IN GRACE of every area of my life that needed to be restored. Following the principles of the course of restoration, reading the books; Seeking the LORD IN A WAY THAT I HAD NEVER MADE.

THE LORD RESTORED ME OF THE LIE OF HAVING BEEN A REJECTED DAUGHTER BY HER MOTHER, AND ABANDONED DAUGHTER BY HER FATHER, AND EVEN FORGOTTEN BECAUSE OF THE DIVORCE OF HIS PARENTS.

HE RESTORED ME, even from have been an adulterous woman that ended with 2 children of that relationship; I almost destroyed a marriage. OH HOW MUCH I LOVE MY HEAVENLY HUSBAND ... I COME TO BE LIKE THE WOMAN WHO BROUGHT THE LORD WITH ALABASTER IN THE HOUSE OF THE TAX COLLECTOR. And it was criticized by the Pharisees that if he knew that the woman was the one who was anointing him, he would not let her touch Him. I was forgiven, cleaned and restored.

And full of love for HIM. AND FOR HIS WORK.

HE (JESUS) GAVE ME A NEW IDENTITY IN HIM AND FOR HIM....

I was myself a concubine, but He restored me and made me a wife for my EH. And the most precious of all, I became HIS Bride ....

After all these areas of my life were restored. AT THE END...

When my HEART WAS COMPLETELY HIS, HE THEN

RESTORED MY MARRIAGE AND EVERY RELATIONSHIP THAT NEEDED TO BE RESTORED!!!!

Today my beloved ERIN!! It will follow the harvest of what you have sown in FERTILE LAND.

YOUR MINISTRY IS FERTILE LAND.

Every woman who is in my Facebook (FB) group and they are already more than 3,300 friends, are being impacted by sharing the RMI Principles with them...

And those women are already testifying to the restoration of their relationship with THE LORD ... And even they have embraced the Principle of MEETING HIM AS THEIR HEAVENLY HUSBAND!!! HALLELUJAH

They have shared that they are knowing true love ...

ETERNAL LOVE, NEVER ENDING LOVE OF A HEAVENLY HUSBAND.

I give GLORY to the LORD FOR YOU, AND FOR YOUR MINISTRY, for your dedication, that you must know. What payment is THERE IS FOR YOUR WORK ... MY BELOVED ERIN.

JEREMIAH 31: 16

This is what the Lord says:

"Restrain your voice from weeping
and your eyes from tears,

for your work will be rewarded,"
Declares the Lord.

I want to share this Word with you my Beloved ERIN...

ISAIAH 62: 2-5
The nations will see your vindication,
and all kings your glory;
you will be called by a new name
that the mouth of the Lord will bestow.
You will be a crown of splendor in the Lord's hand,
a royal diadem in the hand of your God.
No longer will they call you Deserted,
or name your land Desolate.
But you will be called Hephzibah,
and your land Beulah;
for the Lord will take delight in you,
and your land will be married.
As a young man marries a young woman,
so will your Builder marry you;
as a bridegroom rejoices over his bride,
so will your God rejoice over you.

NOTE: HEPHZIBAH - MEANS "MY TREATMENT OR MY COMPLACENCE"

BEULA- MEANS "WOMEN TO MARRY"

THE LORD has been pleased with your work, my beloved. And you will receive the harvest in a short time. And all by Him and for Him ...

I am so thankful for having known the truth that made me free, through your MINISTRY ...

THANK YOU FOR GUIDING ME EVEN THOUGH WE HAVE NEVER SPOKEN A WORD ON THIS JOURNEY I HAD BEEN .... I LISTENED TO YOU, ALWAYS GIVING ME ENCOURAGEMENT!!!!

NOW IS MY TURN TO CHEER YOU UP!!! BE ENCOURAGE, THE BEST IS COMING

THANK YOU ERIN!!!

YOU ARE VERY SPECIAL FOR ME AND FOR ALL THE WOMEN, WHO LIKE ME, THEY KNOWN THE TRUE LOVE THAT EXCEEDS ALL KNOWLEDGE.

I LOVE YOU

RESTORED IN GRACE

~ *Veronica*

Let us REJOICE ALWAYS!!

Veronica lives in California and is Viviana's ePartner. About a year ago Lota, our Spanish Language Minister, contacted us about someone donating books for a women's retreat she was speaking at. It was Veronica.

This testimony is so sweet. Veronica lives in California and is ePartners with Viviana. She was the one that we donated the books to for the women's retreat she was asked to give her testimony. She also heads a Facebook "Restaurada en Gracia" page with over 3,000 followers. She was writing to you Erin because she wanted to share her heart that she is faithful to you and this ministry.

Love,

Lota

On Veronica's FB page she has a note that I believe can encourage many of you, Veronica says....

"Dearly beloved, because more women have been added to the page, and God continues to direct us to urge them to seek only from Him, we sincerely ask you not to contact us by message, know that if you do, we will not be responding, And that is because we do not want to cause you to be unfaithful to God, because in seeking our advice and not the counsel of God, you are unfaithful.

When you spend time with God, Him answering your questions will show you the way. In addition, the time we spend in answering the messages, we can invest in seeking God and continue sharing what He provides. And thus help many more women to seek an intimate relationship with their Heavenly Husband. We do not give counsel, what we do is share some of our testimony, what God has done in our lives, and provide you with the materials that have helped us, which God has used to talk to us.

There are some people who have been offended when they write us telling us details of their problems and talking very badly about their husbands, telling their sins, and asking for advice, and we have only answered that only God can advise them, that they seek Him, because we are nobody. Forgive us for not advising you, but we must not.

Dear ones, only God has the power to make the impossible possible. We would like to be able to embrace you and give them comfort, but even if we tried, we could not, only God can comfort us and give us true peace. Besides, we should not see the sin of others, that is the work of God, not ours. We should rather see our sins and ask God to change us. For you who want to go there telling everyone what is going on, no one can do anything for you or your situation. Go to the only One who can work miracles, Jesus. He is the only one who can and will work miracles in your life if you allow it. Instead of despairing that your situation does not change, try to give everything to God to change them and you .... and fill yourself with His unconditional love. We love you so much. God bless you.

October Encourager post

RESTORED MARRIAGE: VERONICA'S TESTIMONY

How did my Restoration happen?

It all began at the perfect time designed by the LORD. It was over 1 year after my husband left home, and it was not until I discovered that there was someone else occupying his thoughts and desires, that I knew I was losing him, which made me AWAKEN to my reality—that my house and marriage were Destroyed.

And so, without hope, I found hope in THE LORD through your Spanish MINISTRY ayudamatrimonial.com

It was an afternoon coming back from a wedding in the same church where I got married that it began. With those memories of that day where we promised not to separate until death, I looked up in Google the words "marriage aid" and I found THE MINISTRY and the book HOW GOD CAN AND WILL RESTORE YOUR MARRIAGE. Then I listened to the audio in few days, I was so desperate.

I began to seek the LORD 3 times a day and there began my journey to the restoration that I thought would be *only* about my marriage. But not only that was restored, but my life was restored in grace, piece by piece, and in every area in which the LORD began to remind me of and to bring each to light ... I WAS THE CLAY IN HIS HANDS. I did not deny there was a lot of pain, but that same pain was what HE USE to turn my sorrow into JOY....

PSALM 126: 5 "Those who sowed with tears, will reap and rejoice with joyful shouting"...This promise became a reality in my life ... Having been a daughter forgotten by the divorce of my parents, and the abandonment of my father is what gave me the strength not allow my 5 daughters and my eldest son to live the same sad story. That was the push I needed to allow me to surrender to the LORD the work He wanted to do in me—since only HE is able to do it. He made me cry out day and night for help so that the sad story lived in my own childhood would not be repeated.

The LORD began to make me over again after I had shattered myself. With His grace and mercy, He began piece by piece to restore me, to heal me and to wash me in mercy ... He began to bring to my memory my sin in my youth and with great mercy He restored me, cleansing me, with His forgiveness and grace ... And there I can say that I started my LOVE STORY WITH THE LORD ...

NOW AS AN ADULT I AM JUST LIKE THE SINNER WOMAN WASHING HIS FEET WITH HER TEARS AND GIVING EVERYTHING TO THE LORD AND RECEIVING THE FORGIVENESS OF MY SINS, LUKE 7:36-47

This began to revive THAT FIRST LOVE IN ME ... THAT I KNEW WHEN I WAS 14 YEARS OLD ... THAT WAS HOW THE LORD PRESENTED HIMSELF TO ME, AND WITH MY TEARS OF PAIN AND REPENTANCE, HE EXTENDED HIS MERCY TO ME AND IN THAT INSTANT MY HEART AND MY LOVE WERE REAFFIRMED TO ME... FROM THAT INSTANT, I DID NOT WANT TO SEPARATE FROM MY LOVE ... FROM MY ONE AND ONLY TRUE LOVE, JESUS...

Then I could only see my condition and become focused on the complete restoration of my life. THE LORD, He began to show me and to make me know His promises in which I could rest and hold on to during the times of anguish that came (Psalm 119:49). In trials and afflictions, but He always carried me out with His hands. He has never left me since that moment that

I was restored in grace. He began to restore every relationship destroyed in my life, including my relationship with my earthly father, and although we are a long way away, THE LORD directed me, I obeyed, and He made it possible... HE MADE THE REST OF THE WORK... working in the Heart of my father. The Lord allowed me to know the love of a FATHER IN MY HEAVENLY AND ETERNAL FATHER, AND TO KNOW THE LORD TOO AS MY HEAVENLY HUSBAND ... this made my life find the reason to live THROUGH HIM AND FOR HIM... And everything else was added little by little...

Putting a fervent desire in my heart to share HIS love with other women, was how Restored By Grace began, and using the tools of the ministry ayudamatrimonial.com, and adding the remarkable things that He was doing in me and through me ... To GOD BE THE GLORY; He returned my husband home!

But the restoration was not yet complete since THE LORD had much more to take off of me, to teach me how to extract the precious from the evil. Jeremiah 15:19

It was days, weeks, and months that, although they were for me many times eternal, FOR THE LORD was what I needed to build and to restore myself completely. The tests were a preparation to live now FOR THE LORD and for HIS purpose.

Giving fruits of His love, and being able to sow, first in my family, and then to sow in the lives of others, ALL FOR HIS GLORY AND FOR HIS KINGDOM TO EXTEND IN THE EARTH ...

THANKS TO THE LORD FOR HAVING LED ME TO THE MINISTRY OF ERIN THIELE, AND THANKS TO ALL THOSE BRAVE SERVANTS THAT SERVE IN THIS MINISTRY ... THE LORD BLESS YOU ABUNDANCE

VERONICA

Chapter 41

Coke

"…be like a wise man who built his
house on the rock… it did not fall,
because it had been founded on the rock."
—Matthew 7:24-26

"Stand Firm"

First, an email from Coke:

A little over ten years ago I was diagnosed with MS Multiple Sclerosis. My wife left soon after and a friend of mine gave me 2 books - *A Wise Man* and *How God Will Restore your Marriage*. I read both books and learned so much, knowing I wanted to help others. I soon set up a website and even had my email address posted on your website so that I could help other men. Within a month, I had received emails from over 6 countries and 2 dozen states. Unfortunately, my health did not get better and neither did my relationship. I soon had to change some things in my life—mainly my work habits, but I never lost faith about my reconciliation with my wife.

My pastor during the time my wife left was a Godsend. If not for his spiritual leadership and help understanding scripture during my time of restoration, (before I got your materials) I probably would be writing a different letter. He was the pastor of the church I attended and later moved to a small town where he preached for several more years and felt a call to return to the military as a chaplain. He is currently in Afghanistan serving as a chaplain to our soldiers overseas. His knowledge of the Bible is deep and he has the ability to read and understand Greek and Hebrew to seek true original scripture interpretation to prevent taking things out of context much like you've shared in your books.

During my troubled times, he took "*A Wise Man*" and wanted to build a men's Bible study from it because he said it was the best study any man could use to be himself spiritually. However, he ended up moving to another church, nevertheless, I was able to stay in contact with him throughout my restoration journey and visited his church after my wife and I were restored and remarried in November 2009.

I also had my prayer partner during my time of restoration. It was his testimony that gave me hope shortly after my brother passed away with cancer in May of 2005, at the height of my pain and separation from my wife. He is who told me about this ministry where I went to purchase the books he recommended, your books, and thus headed down the same trail he was headed.

His wife had left also. My prayer partner was a "poster child" for what someone should look like that wanted and believed that his marriage was on it's way to restoration! Well it was!! In 2006 his wife came home and they now have a happy marriage with a daughter named Grace, another one of your many restoration babies! These men were vital men placed by God in my life that stood in the gap with me as I went down my trail to restore my marriage.

I was also blessed that my own parents and my children stood beside me and at the top of the list, let me mention them again, were the men above, for without their prayers and faith, it would have been a very tough ride.

Then in November of 2009, as I said above—my wife and I remarried!! Not only was my marriage restored, but my MS is currently in remission AND I have a new job, doing what I love, ranching. The road maps of scripture help me through some really tough times.

When you have a moment, please Holler back!

God Bless your trails!

Coke

"Be the kind of man each morning that when you wake up and your feet hit the floor the devil says "Oh crap, he's up!"

Coke's RESTORED Marriage Testimony:

"Therefore, my beloved brothers, be steadfast, immovable, always abounding in the work for the Lord, knowing that in the Lord your labor is not in vain." 1 Corinthians 15:58 KJV

I was driving home late one night from a rodeo in the summer of 1982 after taking part in a riding competition. The rain was pounding the highway. The drive was slow and I found myself in a deep conversation with my Lord. My heart had been heavy over the last several months about a young woman whom I felt was going to be my partner for life. During my conversation with the Lord, I felt certain that this woman would soon be my wife. The rain became a cleansing revelation to me that I knew beyond all cowboy wisdom, that my Holy Pardoner, Jesus Christ, was about to open a gate into a new pasture for me.

The dirt road to my place was flooded. I quickly realized that the storm had nearly destroyed my home. A tornado had blown the barn over and hail stones had knocked out every window on the north side of my home. All the rooms were flooded as three inches of rain and hail blew into the house. Propane gas vapors filled the house, and all electricity was knocked out. I managed to find one room that still had a bed intact and was dry. I wasn't worried about the propane vapors. The house was well ventilated at this point and everything had been shut off.

I located a dry bedroll and I soon found myself listening to the thunder and lightning as I lay down to rest. I felt a strong peace which affirmed the covenant I was about to enter into with God and my future bride. I slept soundly as the heavens rang out about my heart.

On April 16, 1983, I married Edie. I had been raised by sensible Christian parents. Family issues were simple for a family in an agricultural environment with a God-centered culture. Edie, on the other hand, had grown up under the shadows of an alcoholic father who had created a lifetime of turmoil, resulting in a broken family. But, I was a cowboy! I could do this.

Over the next fifteen years or so, my marriage went through many of the typical ups and downs. Our three children had become the center of our lives. They were becoming strong Christian leaders among their friends. To this day, they remain very close to their Lord and Savior. My cowboying, ranching, rodeoing and teaching duties had put a strain on our marriage. I had become a workaholic.

As the man of the house, I was influenced by the world and had become very different from the man that God wanted me to be. I thought of myself as a great cowboy, and I had a false sense of myself as being a sound man of God.

At this point, I had believed that my house had been built on a rock. My walls were brick and the roof had steel beams for protection overhead. I thought of myself as a good man and for all intents and purposes, the world saw Coke Hopping as a great man. But I had too much pride to see that my ways were destroying my family.

Issues began to arise within our home and slowly, the walls began to crumble. On occasion, the word "divorce" was shouted. On several occasions, my wife left on trips that involved drinking and staying away for several days. A slow pattern of peaks and valleys began in our relationship. Each time, the peaks were higher and the valleys were lower. It was only a matter of time before the valley became a pit.

In early 2000, I was diagnosed with Multiple Sclerosis ("MS"). I had had symptoms two years earlier, but doctors had dismissed the neurological symptoms as having developed from spinal cord injuries from years of bareback riding. The burning sensations down my side were attributed to scar tissue on my spinal column in my neck. I soon found myself in the hospital with MS. Little did I know that this would soon become my very own "thorn in my side" just as the Apostle Paul had to endure.

The MS diagnosis affected my physical and emotional stability. My MS was relapsing/remitting which meant it came and went, but it was possible for the symptoms to worsen with each relapse. Physically, I was doing ok. But heat and stress would kick in, and I would often have to lie on a cot in my office at the end of the day, exhausted. My short-term memory became a constant battle. I dropped things, I tripped over things, I slurred my speech, and I became an angry man. My children could not understand why I was never happy. I argued frequently and lost many friends from my angry outbursts. And I lost the ability to be the man that my wife so desperately needed in her life.

In 2004, my wife was back in her father's life. She was his "little girl". Their relationship had been on and off throughout Edie's youth and sadly it continues in this way to this day. He asked her to become a part of his auction business. My wife finally had a father in her life who took care of her and loved her as a father should, what she had always wanted as a child. Edie began driving back and forth to Amarillo every weekend to work with her father in his auction business. I could see that she was drifting away from me. Our finances started to collapse and I had to approach my father-in-law for help. I talked to him about my relationship with my wife and explained that I was worried because he had become the central figure of a man in her life, not me. He explained that as her father, he was supposed to be the central figure in his daughter's life.

My father-in-law had quit drinking soon after my daughter was born. However, he was still pretty much the same individual except that he no longer drank. Some would describe him as a dry alcoholic. He was a hard man who had lost everything but he had struggled in recent years to build a strong business in the area. He was very well respected in the business world, and he seemed to be walking down a different path, thanks to a new relationship with his church. My father-in-law honestly believed that his relationship with his daughter should be ranked higher than my relationship with her, and he believed this to be sound doctrine. Yet, this was not scriptural. "For this reason a man will leave his father and mother and be united to his wife, and the two will become one flesh." Eph. 5:31 NIV As her husband, I should be the man in Edie's life.

My wife continued to work at the auctions every weekend. In October 2004, I was hospitalized again. My wife brought up the issue of divorce again. It was the perfect time for her to do this. I was in a situation where I could not fight back. It's sort of hard for a cowboy to follow a woman down the hall in a hospital gown with the back split open! Looking back, I can see God shaking his head at the situation I had put myself into.

Things did not change much over the holidays. In February 2005, I left home with my boys to attend the San Antonio Livestock Show and Rodeo. We had several livestock projects entered in the stock show. I recall calling my wife on the phone on Valentine's Day to tell her "I love you." The reply I received was just the opposite. My wife was driving to San Antonio to see her boys, not me, and it became obvious that she was not alone. She showed up at the stock show, watched the boys participate in their events and left soon after. I remember standing in the parking lot, crying and screaming at the devil. I knew he was behind this whole thing. Upon returning home, my wife had packed her bags and left.

Marriage was the first institution God created¬¬, "That is why a man leaves his father and mother and is united to his wife, and they become one flesh." Gen. 2:23–25 NIV, and it is the last institution established in Revelation, "Let us rejoice and be glad and give him glory! For the wedding of the Lamb has come, and his bride has made herself ready. Fine linen, bright and clean, was given her to wear." (Note: Fine linen represents the righteous acts of God's holy people.) Then the angel said to me, "Write this: Blessed are those who are invited to the wedding supper of the Lamb!" And he added,

"These are the true words of God.'"" Rev. 19:7–9 NIV. Satan has had one mission since the Garden of Eden, which is to destroy every marriage that he can. It is his goal to do it and he knows that he is running out of time. It is at the very core of his overall battle plan to destroy mankind, to destroy the marriage covenant of a man and woman with God. Little did I know that my challenge to Satan would turn into the battle it did. It was "game on" and I was not well prepared at all.

In 1985, I had lost a brother to a motorcycle wreck and now in May 2005, my other brother was dying of cancer. I was working at the Sankey Rodeo School in New Caney, Texas, as a Saddle Bronc instructor when I received the call that my brother had passed away. As I drove home with my boys, I really missed my wife and thought that this situation would surely kick-start our reconciliation. It did not. In fact, my wife did not even sit anywhere close to me. It was clear to everyone that she was not part of my life. I tried to act pitiful and I did indeed look pitiful. I'm also sure that I looked pitiful to everyone else, including my children.

At this point, my wife had moved out, changed addresses, was partying in the town her father lived, and was pretty much out of my life. I had told my two teenage boys that their mother was not coming home. The youngest just shrugged his shoulders and said she was never here anyway. My attempt to get the boys to tell their mom to come home did not work. And I know that it was wrong of me.

It was at this funeral that a long-time friend showed up to pay his last respects. I have known Brice since he was old enough to walk and carry a rope. As a 10-year-old little boy, he had attended Texas Tech football games with me while I was the Texas Tech Masked Rider in 1979 and 1980. Brice called me the following day and I brought him up to date on what had happened in the past year. To this day, I still recall his joyful attitude. His confidence was off the charts. AND to top it off, his wife had separated from him and she was living in Dallas.

Brice explained to me that he had been given two books—*A Wise Man* and *How God Will Restore your Marriage*. He told me about the internet site for men Encouraging Men and he directed me to find it. I told him that I only wanted to read what was true about divorce and marriage from the bible. He quickly explained that the books were not commentaries *about* marriage, but rather, roadmaps to the relevant scriptures throughout the bible. Every question I asked Brice, he always answered with scripture just the way your books do. Jesus did the same thing when he was tempted on the mountain.

Jesus had replied to Satan's temptation three times with "It is written..." Matt 4:5–10 NKJV. Brice described his situation with his wife and how their separation had happened. Every time I talked to Brice, he always spoke positively and was upbeat about his wife's return. And he also talked about how we would all go to Applebee's for a chocolate shake when my wife returned! All I could think of was how hurt Brice was going to be in the end when it didn't happen.

His wife had an apartment and a good job. Brice immediately became my prayer partner never thinking of himself. I remember Brice praying with me as his horseshoeing hammer pounded horseshoe nails into the horse hooves. Whenever I asked how it was going with him, his reply would be, "Great, living the good life! Can't wait for my wife to return home!" Though I know that's not how it was in reality.

The summer was tough. My wife had changed her residence so that after six months, she could divorce me from the county she lived in. She was working for her father. I found out later that her father had paid for her divorce lawyer. My wife had also developed a relationship with one of his employees who would later lead her down very dangerous paths. My father-in-law went to church and was given a book by his pastor that supported the doctrine of divorce. My wife gave me a copy of the book and another copy to my oldest son. I quickly went to my pastor, Dewayne. My pastor quickly showed me the errors in the so-called manual. It was false doctrine presented by wolves in sheep's clothing. "For the LORD God of Israel says That He hates divorce, For it covers one's garment with violence," Says the LORD of hosts. Mal. 2:16 NKJV

The manual on divorce had originated from a Baptist seminary in Louisiana. I called the university and I was eventually directed to a professor who explained that the paper had been written by a student as research for his PhD. The student had been told that if the paper's contents were stated as being doctrine from the bible, it would not receive a passing grade. Somehow, the paper had made its way out of the university and into several churches. Now, it was floating around churches supporting the interpretation that any divorce was biblical!! Be careful. "But there were also false prophets among the people, even as there will be false teachers among you, who will secretly bring in destructive heresies, even denying the Lord who bought them, and bring on themselves swift destruction. And many will follow their destructive ways, because of whom the way of truth will be blasphemed. By covetousness they will exploit you with deceptive words; for a long time their judgment has not been idle, and their destruction does not slumber." 2 Peter 2:1–3 NKJV. Sometimes churches and counselors can do a lot of harm and will some day be accountable for what they've done to cause the innocent to stumble.

My wife and I sought Christian counseling for a short period, what a mistake. The counselor suggested that my wife go see a psychiatrist. Edie went and the psychiatrist diagnosed her as suffering from Borderline Personality Disorder ("BPD"). The session quickly turned to how I should act for my wife and it turned my wife off. The talks did nothing more than talk and blame. The woman who was our counselor said she was a Christian, but she was clearly way off scripturally in how to treat our situation.

In June 2005, I hired a lawyer, since my wife already had a lawyer representing her. Naturally, I thought I had to protect myself. Brice told me one day to get rid of my lawyer. I replied that I would lose the ranch. He quickly explained that I could not serve two masters. "No one can serve two masters. Either you will hate the one and love the other, or you will be devoted to the one and despise the other. You cannot serve both God and money." Matt. 6:24 NIV I could not pray on one hand for my wife to come home, and on the other hand, PAY a lawyer to fight for me in court. My lawyer had already won alimony payment of $500 per month for me to help with my two boys at home. My wife was already two months behind and was about to be hit with a summons that stated the amount was going to be deducted from her paycheck. I was doubtful about this issue for a long time. I had been served divorce papers and all hope seemed to be slipping away.

On many nights, I retreated to a pasture at our ranch where a ridge looked over a small creek known as Indian Creek. I spent many nights praying on this ridge and the bridge over Indian Creek that led to our ranch. I realized in August that I had to step out in faith and release my lawyer. I visited my daughter and my oldest son and explained the situation. I had earlier mailed the signed alimony settlement to my lawyer to start the process of collecting funds. I told my children that I just could not do it and that I was going to call the lawyer and instruct him to withdraw the papers and to withdraw from representing me. My children and I prayed together that Sunday evening.

On the following Monday morning, my daughter called to inform me that she had received a $500 gift from someone in her office for her real estate class tuition. We were excited. I called the lawyer and told him of my plans and he reluctantly agreed. By the end of the week, I had contacted my lawyer numerous times and he never received the signed court papers in the mail! God's plan was in motion!

Over the next several months, I received calls from my wife demanding that I come to court. In Texas, a spouse can get a divorce without the other spouse. I knew that my wife just wanted to fight with me. The divorce was inevitable. I was served papers and I took them out to the pasture and burned them at the foot of a cross that I had set up to pray at. I received a cell phone call one afternoon while I was on horseback from a court officer telling me that I had to be in court the next morning at 9 a.m. I said, "No sir, I don't." He soon became very angry and said that it was my duty to come in. I just simply kept riding across the pasture and said, "Nope". He said that my wife could get everything. I just said, "Don't think so." Now he was mad! And he didn't even have anything invested. I never went to court and I never signed anything. I just looked over at the other cowboy with me and smiled and we rode off into the sunset. (Do note that divorce laws vary state to state.)

Over the course of my journey I made many mistakes, especially over the many months after that. I made the mistake of pursuing my wife when I should not have, which revealed things that God was trying to protect me from knowing about. And it created issues for forgiveness when my spouse returned home. My wife was still involved with the other man ("OM"). She had a job in her new town and she was able to secure 100% financing for a new home. I told Brice all about these new developments about my now divorced relationship and he simply said that she would lose her job, she would lose her house, and she would even get sick. All these things did in fact happen and my wife went down a very dark and tough trail. And once again, her father abandoned her.

Please note: In the case of men's restoration almost in all cases a crisis hits, sometimes several, that leads the wife to return to the husband for help. It's then that the husband, if he is spiritually strong enough, will be there to step in to express his love.

I quickly learned that I did not need to pray for Satan to leave her. Our prayers are powerful and they work. Each time I prayed for Satan to leave my wife, he did. Often times, my wife would call me and be sad about our situation and want to come home, but Satan would return and find her house clean without the Holy Spirit for her protection and he would come back seven times worse and this was literally destroying my wife spiritually, emotionally and physically. "When an impure spirit comes out of a person, it goes through arid places seeking rest and does not find it. Then it says, 'I will return to the house I left.' When it arrives, it finds the house swept clean and put in order. Then it goes and takes seven other spirits more wicked than itself, and they go in and live there. And the final condition of that person is worse than the first." Luke 11:24–26 NIV I soon learned to instead pray a hedge of thorns around her as Hosea did for Gomer. "Therefore I will block her path with thornbushes; I will wall her in so that she cannot find her way." Hosea 2:6 NIV This is what this ministry teaches and it's correct.

In 2006, there were several instances when my wife wanted to reconcile and once, we even bought wedding rings. This too, went south. When we were purchasing the rings, I had a feeling of unease. Sure enough, the OM was not far behind.

This ole cowboy was sure enough in love with his wife, but I wasn't listening to God during this time. I was not reading scripture and seeking wisdom from what I read. So, I continued to check up on my wife and found out more things that God was trying to protect me from. I was like a dog in a fight with a porcupine, I just kept going back for more needles! Ever try to remove porcupine quills from a dog?

Brice never stopped "standing in the gap" and I never stopped having faith that my wife would return. But I had to develop discipline to stay in the Word.

2006 came and went. My rodeo company was doing ok. My teaching job was ok. Our divorce had not affected our ranch and home. But the stress and physical demands of my job and the rodeos was affecting my MS condition. There were several issues with the OM and my wife. He was constantly in trouble with the law and my wife was headed down a dangerous trail with him. The year ended with our family, including my wife, going on a cruise. All three of my children went as well as my future son-in-law. The trip was five days long. The cruise was nice. My wife and I got along fine. But it was obvious that her heart was somewhere else.

On the other hand, Brice was experiencing a restored marriage with his wife. His wife had moved back to their home! Unfortunately he never wrote it down, much like so many others who experience a restored marriage, most don't take the time to share it.

The new year was going to be better. I knew that my time as a teacher was coming to a close. The MS was making it harder and harder to get through the day. I soon put in my retirement notice and I was able to leave school in

March 2007 with enough days accumulated so that I could get paid until June. A new job opportunity came up and I moved to the College Station Area. I put the ranch up for sale and my youngest son moved south with me. My daughter had just graduated from Texas A&M and my oldest son was attending Texas A&M.

2007 came in with me gaining new faith in restoration. The turning point literally came when I took my eyes off my wife and placed them on my Lord and Savior. I let go. I stepped out of what the worldly zone of emotions was telling me. I begin focusing on scripture and on my relationship with the Lord. I fasted more to get closer to the Lord and feel His presence. I was finally willing to let God take control of my life.

By now, my books, *The Holy Bible*, *A Wise Man* and *How God Will Restore your Marriage* paperback books were worn out. My roadmap through the bible was more clear and my priority became God first, not my wife. But best of all, I gained a new perspective of reading scripture and a new relationship with my ole Holy Pardoner!

MS was still an issue in my life. One thing that resulted from my struggle with MS was the softening of my heart. God had softened my stance on some old tough guy cowboy attitudes. I went back to several old friends that I had blown up at and asked for their forgiveness. This act also showed me that I was also supposed to forgive my wife. "Then Peter came to Jesus and asked, "Lord, how many times shall I forgive my brother or sister who sins against me? Up to seven times?" Jesus answered, "I tell you, not seven times, but seventy-seven times. Therefore, the kingdom of heaven is like a king who wanted to settle accounts with his servants."" Matt 18:21–23 NIV And this meant that I had to forgive daily!

My actions in the early years had set the stage for the demise of my marriage. Yes, my wife had inherited a curse from an alcoholic parent and had parents who were divorced. However, scripture also shows that blessings can break curses. That was my job as a husband and head of the house. We men underestimate the role that we are called to hold as head of the house. The husband is commanded to love his wife. "Husbands, love your wives, just as Christ loved the church and gave himself up for her to make her holy, cleansing her by the washing with water through the word." Eph. 5:25–26 NIV

The husband is instructed to treat his wife as an equal heir. "Husbands, in the same way be considerate as you live with your wives, and treat them with respect as the weaker partner and as heirs with you of the gracious gift of life, so that nothing will hinder your prayers." 1 Peter 3:7–8 NIV

My physical home had been destroyed and the walls washed away, but my very existence stood on a Rock. That principle is the foundational scripture that starts you down a trail to restore your marriage. Even your Wise Man and Wise Woman starts with that principle. To make it through the cacti, rattlesnakes, droughts, cows running off, and getting bucked off your horse, you will need the very Word of God to guide you on the trail that Jesus wants you to walk down. Most people will submit to the ways of the world and after a period of time, they will give in to the ways of this world and do what the latest reality show says AND they will never see restoration in their lives. Ask Job from the Old Testament. It does not say how long his ordeal took. Ask Hosea from the Old Testament. It doesn't say how long Hosea had to wait until he was instructed to go back into town and acquire his wife Gomer.

Looking back and reflecting on my restoration process, it is easy to see the signs that I was getting close to restoration, since I now have 20/20 hindsight. I think one of the hardest things for most people is to have 20/20 foresight.

Things starting falling apart in my wife's life in the spring of 2007 when she injured her back at work which made it difficult for her to work, resulting in issues with her ability to pay the mortgage for her house. All I could do was just be there to answer the phone in a positive spirit, but I did not give her money because I knew that that was not what God wanted me to do. I'd spoken to Him, willing to do so, but He told me not to. I did help several times to repair stuff around her house, although I saw evidence of the OM's stuff which was tough. At the end, when I moved my wife's belongings back to my home, I only moved her stuff. I'm sure some homeless person benefited from the stuff that was left on the curb.

The biggest thing I remember about this time period was not so much what my wife was doing but "where my heart was with the Lord." I had a sense of peace, and the feeling of panic that I had whenever my wife went left or right, did not affect me as it had in the beginning.

This can be a dangerous time in the restoration process. It creates a sense of "OK, I don't think I want her back now, or I can live without her!" I always tell men to BE CAREFUL! Satan is now moving the pendulum back the other way. He knows he is losing the battle. Remember the scripture above from Hosea—God said that He would return Hosea's wife and HE (God) would remove the mouths of Baal from her. When this process starts, stay the course and let God finish His work and be prepared to accept your wife when she returns. If you don't, then it will be you who has turned your back on the marriage covenant that you entered into, as God is restoring your marriage. The whole Book of Hosea is about the adulterous relationship of God's chosen people with their Lord and we are to be the living example now.

The turning point for my restoration came when my heart became peaceful with my relationship with God. I felt a sense of "Ok, I'm going to be OK." I also recall feeling or thinking it was ok to move on without my wife. That's when I had to stop and battle this. I think lots of couples do this and for this reason, I think that is why there are a lot of marriages that are not restored. The spouse that leaves will say something like "I don't love you anymore and I never will! SO move on!" And the spouse, the one on the receiving end of this comment, usually hangs in for about 10 months. This almost happened to me too. Though we are to move on with our lives, developing our relationship with Him, moving on and remarrying is adultery, plan and simple. Erin did a good job of finding the scriptures if you're searching for the truth. Just read *How God Will Restore your Marriage* if you really want the truth on this subject.

Little did I know about all the little things that God was doing in my wife's heart. Had I moved on, I would not have been able to see the Holy Spirit flow from my wife's heart and mouth today as she now gives praise and honor to her Savior! My turning point came about after two years. As I look back, it seemed to play out in phases that mostly paralleled my walk with Jesus.

My restoration happened in January 2007 when I had to make some changes in my job. My health was starting to affect my work and could have been due to the stress from my marriage. Nonetheless, I knew I had to do something. As I started to move in a positive direction to fix things, I tried to do it in a way, which reflected a new me, a new Coke. I took my clothes to get pressed at the laundromat, I dressed in clean clothes and tried to improve my "first impression image" every day. I tried to look positive and if I was having a bad day, I tried to fake it until I really felt positive.

When it came time to move, my wife contacted me and wanted to move with me. I was happy that she was ready to load up in my covered wagon as we moved to a different ranch. Things were pretty good. At first, I believe my wife moved because my boys were moving with me. It became obvious on a couple of occasions when I found stuff from the OM that she had still been in contact with him. This is a tough time for lots of relationships that He restores, I am sure of that. It was tough for me. But I learned I had to wait for Him to complete the process.

It was obvious from what I saw where the OM's heart was and how Satan was pulling his strings. I could see very easily that this was not a man of God and this one fact gave me confidence that my Lord would prevail. I also think that knowing this kept me from doing anything stupid. I remember telling my wife at this point that we were leaving Sodom and Gomorrah and that I could not look back at my past sins and that if she did, I could not look back to help her. This was tough, but I also did my best to do it with a loving heart. Lot's wife looked back because she missed her past and she was turned into a pillar of Salt. (Gen. 19:21–26 NKJV)

Each man has his own trail to walk. Each man will journey down a different path that leads through different canyons and over different mountains. I tell you that scripture never changes and never contradicts itself. Some say you can read the bible a hundred times and it will tell you a hundred different things each time. Not true! The Word is, and always will be, the same yesterday, today and forever!

Go out under a tree and place a plumb bob hanging from a tree limb so that it's barely touching the soft sand underneath it. Gently move the plumb bob to one side or the other so that it makes scratch marks in the sand as it moves back and forth. Watch it move back and forth and sooner or later, the plumb bob will come to a complete stop at the BOTTOM DEAD CENTER every time. That is His Word! The Word may speak to you differently each time you read it, and it should. As for those scratch marks outside the center point, they are similar to how you interpret the Word to meet your own wishes. It is the living Word and it will speak to you, but you will need to understand true doctrine to keep the plumb bob centered. Because of the Holy Spirit that remains here after Jesus ascended to Heaven in the Book of Acts, the Word will speak to you like no other book. It never changes! It never contradicts itself! It has withstood thousands of years of interpretation! AND numerous authors wrote it over hundreds and hundreds of years apart from each other. There is a reason why it is called the Holy Bible—It is the very WORD of God that was spoken and recorded by a very special group of writers! This is what I love about being part of this ministry, it's based on the Word alone. It doesn't say what you want to hear or what some denomination says, it is bible based, period.

What's true too is that each man will have a different journey and each man will develop his own testimony. A friend of mine went through a similar set of circumstances as I did. He fought for restoration for about a year but then felt like he could remarry. So he remarried and had another child. Then one day, his ex-wife returned after five years and she commented that if he had waited, she would have gotten back together with him. Sadly, she went off and has been with several men that has adversely affected his children and the new life he was hoping to make with his new wife (who I heard is laying on a bed of sickness as Revelation 2:22 warns will happen). This friend of mine is now in another marriage with another woman and another child. He told me later that looking back, waiting five years was not a very long time to wait. But he had already remarried twice.

If we would just wake up and realize the destruction of marriages falling around us, and remarriages running rampant through His believers, it's horribly sad. God gives each of us the tools we need and His promise of Salvation and Restoration and it never changes throughout the scriptures. So why do you think that your situation would turn out any differently? You must have faith and the Lord does allow for you to pray for faith. But there will come a time that we all must act on that faith! Saddle up whatever bronc the Lord has given you. Some of you will get bucked off. Some of you will make a great 8-second ride and then jump off with so much pride that in the end you will fall flat on your face as you walk out of the arena. And some of you may even get on a donkey, just as Lord did when he rode into Jerusalem for the Passover. But in the end, I promise that the horse you will ride in God's army will be a magnificent animal that you will ride next to Jesus on his Horse. It's time to enter the round pen and select your mounts for the ride ahead. Have faith in your Lord and Savior, and stand firm. If you get bucked off, I say to you, "Get back on!!!"

My wife and I remarried in November 2009. My wife now has a new relationship with Jesus Christ and it is because of our Lord and Savior, Jesus Christ in what He helped me come through. Even though I did have to sell our small ranch, I now manage a much larger ranch that came with a very nice home. I was able to complete my Masters in Agricultural Leadership, Education, and Communications at Texas A&M and I graduated at the same time with my oldest son. My daughter is married and expecting their first child. My youngest son is now in college. My wife teaches 2nd grade now and is anxious to be a grandmother. My MS continues to be in remission.

My home was washed away but not its foundation. I am thankful to my parents for establishing the Christian doctrine in my life. I pray that my life will do the same for my children. John Wayne said in the movie The Cowboys, "It's not how you're buried, it's how you are remembered."

It is your Savior, Jesus Christ who will get you through, nothing and no one else. Let the books and courses this magnificient ministry offers serve as a map to help you find your way through God's Holy Word—The Bible. God will lead you as you become "A Wise Man" building your home on a Rock. "Therefore everyone who hears these words of mine and puts them into practice is like a wise man who built his house on the rock. The rain came down, the streams rose, and the winds blew and beat against that house; yet it did not fall, because it had its foundation on the rock. Matt. 7:24–25 NIV

Stand Firm and may God bless your trails!

~ *Coke and Edie Hopping*

P.S.

Brice, it is time we had that chocolate shake at Applebee's!

UPDATE:

Coke went to be with the Lord. Coke was just 55. He will be greatly missed and trust that the Lord will see fit to send us men to fill his boots—a passionate minister to head up our men's ministry (which He faithfully did by sending us Patrick and Jodi in Australia).

"It's not how you're buried, it's how you are remembered."

Yes, Coke, we will always remember you **and** your courage.

~ *Erin*

As this book got larger and larger we were unable to keep up with printing all of them in a book!

What you have read is just a *small sample* of the POWER and FAITHFULNESS of God that are told through countless restored marriages! We continue to post new restored marriage, and restored relationship testimonies (children, siblings, parents, etc.) on our site each week.

Don't let ANYONE try to convince you that God cannot restore YOUR marriage! It is a lie. The TRUTH is that He is MORE THAN ABLE!!

Is Your Marriage... Crumbling? Hopeless? Or Ended in Divorce?

At Last There's Hope!

Have you been searching for marriage help online? It's not by chance, nor is it by coincidence, that you have this book in your hands. God is leading you to Restore Ministries that began by helping marriages that *appear* hopeless—like yours!

God has heard your cry for help in your marriage struggles and defeats. He predestined this **Divine Appointment** to give you the hope that you so desperately need right now!

We know and understand what you are going through since many of us in our restoration fellowship have a restored marriage and family! No matter what others have told you, your marriage is not hopeless! We know, after filling almost two books of restored marriage testimonies, that God is able to restore any marriage—especially yours!

"Behold, I am the LORD, the God of all flesh; is anything too difficult for Me?" (Jeremiah 32:27).

If you have been told that your marriage is hopeless or that without your husband's help your marriage cannot be restored! Each week we post a new Restored Relationship from one of our Restoration Fellowship Members that we post on our site.

"Ah Lord GOD! Behold, You have made the heavens and the earth by Your great power and by Your outstretched arm! Nothing is too difficult for You"! (Jeremiah 32:17).

If you have been crying out to God for more help, someone who understands, someone you can talk to, then we invite you to join our RMI Restoration Fellowship. Since beginning this fellowship, we have seen more marriages restored on a regular basis than we ever thought possible!

Restoration Fellowship

Restoration is a "narrow road"—look around, most marriages end in divorce! But if your desire is for a restored marriage, then our Restoration Fellowship is designed especially for you!

Since beginning this fellowship, we have seen marriages restored more consistently than we ever thought possible.

Let us help you stay committed to "working with God" to restore your marriages. Restoration Fellowship can offer you the help, guidance, and support you will need to stay on the path that leads to victory—*your* marriage restored!

Let us assure you that all of our marriages were restored by GOD (through His Word) as we sought Him to lead us, teach us, guide us and transform us through His Holy Spirit. This, too, is all you need for *your* marriage to be restored.

However, God continues to lead people to our ministry and fellowship to gain the faith, support and help that so many say that they needed in their time of crisis.

"I want you to know how MUCH the RMI resources, the fellowship and the website have meant to me. Yes, I will candidly say all you NEED is the Word of God to restore your marriage, but RMI shines a brilliant light on that Word with so much encouragement. I really believe that this would be a much longer more painful journey with a LOT more detours if I had not had the resources of RMI to go back to again and again, leading me to a genuine love for God." K.H. in North Carolina

"My husband did not talk to me for the first six months after he left but God continued His faithfulness to help me not give up; He used Restore Ministries to encourage me – I could not have made it without you." Michelle, **Restored** in Wisconsin

"God led me to Restore Ministries, which provided the encouragement I needed at exactly the time I needed it. All of the resources you required for membership helped me. They gave me encouragement, hope and a sense of peace." Stephanie, **Restored** in Kansas

"I cannot thank God enough for His unfailing mercies and for restoring our marriage after five years of marital troubles and separation! I was on the website every day for encouragement. After seeing the changes in me, my husband started to change, he held me and told me he was sorry for all that happened, that that he loved me and always did despite everything!" Lina, **Restored** in Ghana

Join our Restoration Fellowship TODAY and allow us to help YOU **restore** YOUR marriage.

Like What You've Read?

If you've been blessed by this book
get the full WOTT Series available
on EncouragingBookstore.com & Amazon.com

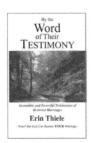

By the Word of Their Testimony (Book 1): *Incredible and Powerful Testimonies of Restored Marriages*

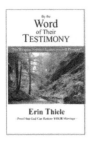

By the Word of Their Testimony (Book 2): *No Weapon Formed Against you will Prosper*

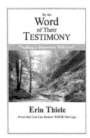

By the Word of Their Testimony (Book 3): *Nothing is Impossible With God*

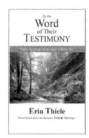

Word of Their Testimony (Book 4): *Take up your cross and follow Me*

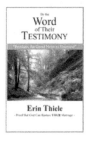

Word of Their Testimony (Book 6): *Proclaim the Good News to Everyone*

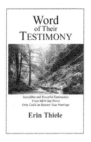

Word of Their Testimony: *Incredible and Powerful Testimonies of Restored Marriages From Men*

Mentioned in this Book

Also available
on EncouragingBookstore.com & Amazon.com

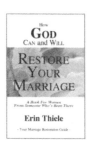

How God Can and Will Restore Your Marriage:
From Someone Who's Been There

A Wise Woman: *A Wise Woman Builds Her House*
By a FOOL Who First Built on Sinking Sand

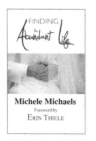

Finding the Abundant Life *by Michele Michaels*

Restore Ministries International

POB 830
Ozark, MO 65721
USA

For more help
Please visit one of our Websites:

EncouragingWomen.org

HopeAtLast.com

RestoreMinistries.net

RMIEW.com

AjudaMatrimonial.com (Portuguese)

AyudaMatrimonial.com (Spanish)

Zachranamanzelstva.com (Slovakian)

Aidemaritale.com (French)

Uiteindelikhoop.com (Afrikaans)

EncouragingMen.org

Made in the USA
Middletown, DE
05 September 2022